THE STUDY OF POLITICS:
THE WESTERN TRADITION
AND AMERICAN ORIGINS

**FOUNDATIONS OF AMERICAN GOVERNMENT
AND POLITICAL SCIENCE**

Joseph P. Harris, Consulting Editor

Revisions and additions have been made to keep this series up to date and to enlarge its scope, but its purpose remains the same as it was on first publication: To provide a group of relatively short treatises dealing with major aspects of government in modern society. Each volume introduces the reader to a major field of political science through a discussion of important issues, problems, processes, and forces and includes at the same time an account of American political institutions. The author of each work is a distinguished scholar who specializes in and teaches the subjects covered. Together the volumes are well adapted to serving the needs of introductory courses in American government and political science.

THE STUDY OF POLITICS:
THE WESTERN TRADITION
AND AMERICAN ORIGINS

SECOND EDITION

ANDREW HACKER, 1973,
QUEENS COLLEGE
THE CITY UNIVERSITY OF NEW YORK

McGraw-Hill Book Company
New York   San Francisco   St. Louis   Düsseldorf   Johannesburg
Kuala Lumpur   London   Mexico   Montreal   New Delhi   Panama
Rio de Janeiro   Singapore   Sydney   Toronto

This book was set in Helvetica by Rocappi, Inc. The editors were Robert P. Rainier and Ronald Q. Lewton, the designer was Janet Bollow, and the production supervisor was Michael A. Ungersma. The drawings were done by Judith L. McCarty.

The printer and binder was The Book Press.

THE STUDY OF POLITICS: THE WESTERN TRADITION AND AMERICAN ORIGINS

Library of Congress Cataloging in Publication Data

Hacker, Andrew.
  The study of politics.

  Bibliography: p. 00
  1. Political science.—History. 2. Political science—History–United States. I. Title.
JA81.H233 1973   320'.09   72-4851
ISBN 0-07-025395-1
ISBN 0-07-025394-3 (pbk.)

1234567890 BPBP 79876543

PREFACE

This revised and expanded edition of *The Study of Politics* seeks to show undergraduates the kinds of questions which need to be asked for an understanding of political life. The introductory chapter outlines the major emphases of the discipline, and new material has been added on recent approaches to political research.

Part I summarizes the enduring issues of political theory: the great questions the Western tradition has posed and sought to answer. These are best expressed in the literature of that heritage; and for this reason at least passing reference is made to the books and authors that have contributed to this stream of ideas. The sections dealing with political conflict and the quest for equality receive more extended treatment in this edition, as does the question of whether a society can be transformed by working within a constituted system. The book stresses that theoretical abstractions must be interwoven with a knowledge of institutional functioning and human behavior.

Part II, therefore, focuses chiefly on such a synthesis: the *Federalist* papers of James Madison and Alexander Hamilton which were written in support of the newly drafted Constitution. Their analysis embraces a science of human nature, a philosophy of the good society, and an explanation of how the American system would operate in that context. An entirely new chapter draws on the ideas of Thomas Jefferson, whose commitment to democratic values stood in marked contrast to those of the *Federalist* authors. Most of the controversies in contemporary American politics reflect the opposing assumptions of these three figures. If Madison, Hamilton, and Jefferson were intensely involved in the problems of their time, they also demonstrated that it is possible to assume a scientific and philosophical posture even in the midst of ideological conflict. They comprise a model that any student of politics would do well to emulate.

ANDREW HACKER

CONTENTS

THE STUDY OF POLITICS:
THE WESTERN TRADITION
AND AMERICAN ORIGINS

1 THE STUDY OF POLITICS

Basic to democracy is the right of every citizen to express political opinions. Men have fought—and are still fighting—for this fundamental freedom, and it is one that is never abandoned voluntarily. Moreover, each citizen creates for himself his own perception of political reality. That is, his view of politics is based on his own experience and preconceptions; moreover, most of us are convinced that we see things as they really are. The bank president and the garage mechanic, the bishop and the plumber, are all prepared to discourse on politics without much urging. Nor should this be surprising.

EQUAL VOTES
AND EQUAL OPINIONS

In a democracy every adult citizen has the right to vote, and to this extent to exercise a share of power equal to that of any other citizen. The public is asked to select the men and women who are to govern, a not unsubstantial responsibility. Yet no tests of knowledge or intelligence must be passed to acquire the vote. All that is required is to have reached the age of eighteen and not to be a convicted felon or an inmate of a mental institution. Not only is passing an examination in political science unnecessary, but no evidence need be given that the voter has studied or reflected on political affairs. It is assumed that even the most average of citizens will know how he wants to be governed and who he wants to govern him. For, it has been observed, he is the one who wears the shoe and he knows where it pinches.

The citizen is flattered by this compliment democracy pays to him. (Some say the flattery goes to his head.) If he has the right to vote, the reasoning proceeds, he has the right to assume that his political knowledge is correct and his political opinions are sound. Woe unto the elected official who insists on telling his constituents they are ignorant or misguided in their thinking. He may educate them to the acceptance of new ideas, and many politicians have accomplished this manful feat. But it is a long and cautious process, and such education must never appear to upset beliefs that are cherished or prejudices that are deeply held.

THE PLIGHT OF THE EXPERT   Can there be "experts" in a society which purports to be democratic? Can a country where the majority rules admit that there are, in its midst, persons having superior political knowledge? To grant this is to suggest that there can be individuals whose opinions carry greater validity than those of their neighbors. This is a perplexing question, and one that has preoccupied philosophers for more than 2,000 years. But if the problem bothers philosophers, it does not usually trouble the typical truck driver. For, as has been pointed out, the average citizen shows little inclination to turn over his vote to someone who is supposedly better qualified to use it. By the same token, he will not remain quiet when politics is being discussed. For he is unwilling to admit that his opinions are inferior to anyone else's.

Thus the expert faces difficulty when he seeks to establish his credentials. For his audience (if he has one) will ask: "What do *you* know that we don't know?" It is worth taking a moment to ponder whether there is a satisfactory answer to this question. Rare indeed is the political expert who can convince others that his researches have given him greater knowledge of political reality; for it is by no means easy to persuade others that his judgments on political policies are somehow sounder than those conventionally held. The audience is usually skeptical, and often not a little annoyed at such pretensions. Although the expert may be smart, they also know that he—like them—has only one vote.

UNLEARNING THE OBVIOUS All this needs to be underlined because every year several hundred thousand Americans enroll in courses in political science. In doing this they are embarking on a process whereby they will become substantially more expert on the subject of politics than the average citizen. What are they about to learn?

They are, first and foremost, unlearning. They will discover very early in the season that the knowledge and opinions they have brought to college are highly unreliable. We are all, no matter what our backgrounds, raised in a comfortable and comforting world of illusions. We see only what we want to see and we believe what we want to believe. (Psychologists call this "selective perception.") An academic setting is the best place to dispel these illusions. For the college student is, for all intents and purposes, in a period of suspended animation. Father's dinner-table dicta on the latest mischiefs perpetrated by the men who govern us must now face competition from other sources. The Sunday visits of Uncle Jim, a successful businessman who seems to know all about what Congress should do and the Supreme Court not do, seem less authoritative. For confronting Father and Uncle Jim are professors—men and women with new ideas that are bound to run counter to those that prevailed at home. Furthermore, the college student has several years of freedom before he must begin to support himself by earning a living. This is a welcome respite, not least for developing an understanding of politics. For once one is in possession of a wife (or a husband) and a family (or a job), the inevitable tendency is to view politics as it affects one's immediate interests. The citizen who is weighed down with personal ambitions and responsibilities is apt to extrapolate political generalizations from his immediate experiences. In other words, he is apt to assume that policies which benefit him are best for the entire nation.

OVERCOMING IDEOLOGY   The college setting is, to be sure, a sheltered one. But it is a shelter from the prejudices of the family dinner table and interests that become ingrained later in life. Perhaps the best way to describe the matter is to say that most political knowledge and most political opinions are actually *ideology*. This term requires some explanation.

Ideology can take two forms. On the one hand, ideology is a *distorted* perception of political reality. An individual may believe that his knowledge of politics is altogether valid, that things are in fact as he believes them to be. However, these perceptions all too often suffer from distortions; they tend to be inaccurate because people tend to absorb the information they wish to hear. Everyone, for example, has a notion of what life is like in Cuba. Or everyone assumes he knows whether or not malnutrition is a serious problem at this time. But how many of us really know how many people have been executed or imprisoned in Cuba; or how many people are actually hungry in our own country? The odds are that few of us have such information. Nevertheless, we continue to assume that our knowledge of these conditions is correct knowledge. In other words, the pictures in our heads are ideologies: distorted images of reality.

In addition, ideology is a *rationalization* of political arrangements we would either like to see continued or would like to see come into being. Man is a complicated creature, and not the least of his charms is his ability to rationalize. Suppose you encounter Jones hitting Smith over the head with a lead pipe. If you ask Jones why he is denting Smith's cranium, it is highly doubtful that he will reply, "I am doing this because I enjoy it." On the contrary, Jones will explain to you that the lead-pipe treatment is actually for Smith's own good—whether Smith realizes that or not. Alternately, he may claim that subduing Smith is for the greater good of society. Our political discourse runs along similar ideological lines. We persuade ourselves that policies that benefit us augment the welfare of the whole country. A businessman asserts that he must be permitted higher profits so he can invest them in the stock market, thus contributing to economic progress. The trade union member, on the other hand, demands a substantial raise in wages, claiming that his increased purchasing power will create more jobs and hence make for a prosperous economy. In actual fact the businessman wants the extra cash for a Florida vacation and the trade unionist wants his raise for similar, if less extravagant, reasons. But for each to get what he wants he must persuade others that these wants spring from lofty motives. So they invent rationalizations. If truth be known, most talk of "principles" is in fact ideology. By the same token, composite outlooks such as "liberalism" and "conservatism" can be seen as at least in part distortions of reality and rationalizations for particular aspirations and interests.

IS POLITICS A SCIENCE?

The study of politics involves acquiring specialized knowledge. This knowledge, if it is to be taken seriously, cannot be secured in a haphazard way. As has been pointed out, the average person's store of political information comes from his "selective perception" of the events and personalities around him. Relying on facts that seem to him most significant, he will conclude that labor unions are corrupt, that the Republican party is dominated by big business, or that people on welfare prefer not to work. However, if generalizations such as these are distortions of reality, an accurate understanding can only result from a systematic examination of political life.

The study of politics is not a "science" in the sense that chemistry, physics, and biology are. The traditional sciences rely on controlled experiments, conducted in a laboratory setting. It is not possible to lock up politicians in a laboratory as if they were guinea pigs, nor is it possible to impose precise laboratory conditions on the political arenas of real political life. (Imagine asking a candidate to "experiment" in his use of various campaign techniques, to see if perhaps some might be dispensed with. His reply will show that politicians have no desire to run in experimental mazes.) Moreover, the chemist or biologist can assume a dispassionate view toward the materials with which he works. The amoeba and the atom can be regarded disinterestedly, the scientist having no emotional interest in whether they wiggle or split or lie still. The student of politics, on the other hand, may find himself deeply involved with his subject matter. Whether he acknowledges the fact or not, he will look on some people and policies as good and on others as less than praiseworthy. Such an involvement runs the risk of introducing some strains of subjectivity into his analysis.

The term "political science" must therefore be used in a rather loose way. But not too loosely. The real question is which facts, and what arrangements of facts, are admissible in drawing conclusions. To say that one gathers and organizes facts in a systematic (or "scientific") way is to say that the *method* one uses is important.

SCIENCE IN THE SUBURBS   The residents of the communities surrounding Central City have, over the past several years, been voting down proposals for school-bond issues. Professors Whitcomb and Brody, two political scientists at Central College, decide to find out why so many of these referenda have been taking a negative turn. Two nearby towns are chosen for investigation. Whitcomb and his students will study Eastdale, and Brody's team will concentrate on Lakeside. However, before going their separate ways, Whitcomb and Brody must reach agreement on the *methods* they will use in conducting their research. Even before interviewers begin ringing doorbells, the two professors come to several important decisions on the procedures that will be uniformly employed by all members of both research teams. Some of these are: Which voters are to be interviewed? (A common sampling method must be decided upon.) What sorts of questions will be asked? (A uniform questionnaire will have to be prepared.) When should the interviews take place? (During the daytime, when only the women are at home, or in the evening, when husbands can be questioned as well as the wives?)

In doing this, Whitcomb and Brody are ensuring that by using similar approaches they will be obtaining the same information for both Eastdale and Lakeside. Only if this is done can it be said that the facts they gather in the two communities are more than simply the casual impressions of several interviewers. Because close attention has been paid to questions of method, the Whitcomb-Brody survey will be based upon systematic *data* of political behavior. Not all facts or items of information can be called data. This term applies only to findings that have been secured by reliable methods. (Gallup Polls, census statistics, and other carefully designed studies contain data. A taxi-driver's account of his passengers' opinions seldom meets this test.) Thus it may be assumed that if or when some entirely different political scientists conduct a follow-up survey, they will come up with findings similar to those obtained by Whitcomb and Brody. This is not to say that a suburb can be turned into a scientific laboratory. But it is to suggest that some experimental methods can be used in the study of living people and their political behavior.

FACTS OR VALUES?   But having a systematic methodology is not the whole story. Suppose that Whitcomb and Brody happen to hold the personal opinion that too much money is being spent on suburban education. Thus when analyzing their data, they may tend to look upon the rejection of bond issues as rational actions by informed citizens. If, for example, one of their respondents said that he opposed the bonds because he believed that two swimming pools for the high school were an unnecessary luxury, Whitcomb's or Brody's impulse might be to take such a reply at its face value. Yet the remark about swimming pools might be a surface expression of other, less easily articulated, reasons.

However, over at Central State University two other political scientists, Professors Burton and Caldwell, have some doubts about the validity of the Whitcomb-Brody findings. So they decide to do another study (called a "replication") of the Eastdale and Lakeside referenda. However, this second team may, for their part, enter into their research with the assumption that the suburban voters were shortsighted or misguided when they voted down the school-bond issues. Even though Burton and Caldwell employ the identical sampling and interview methods as did Whitcomb and Brody, their report nevertheless concludes that the voters of Eastdale and Lakeside were basically nonrational in their behavior. Instead of taking seriously the reasons offered by the people they interviewed, Burton and Caldwell conclude that social strains, psychological insecurity, and racial tensions are the crucial factors in shaping bond-issue voting behavior.

Which of these two studies has the "correct" interpretation? The response must be that all four of these researchers—Burton and Caldwell no less than Whitcomb and Brody—were guilty of allowing their personal values to affect their research results. Although some of the conclusions arrived at in both of the studies may be interesting, each one ends up being but a partial—and a distorted—depiction of suburban political reality. There are several ways to prevent the intrusion of subjectivity. The first is for the student himself to become conscious of his own opinions and preferences. Then he can constantly ask himself if he is seeing what he wants to see, or whether he is seeing what is really there. Most people do not have such an insight into their own prejudices, but a serious student of politics must develop this self-awareness.

Moreover, bias can also be reflected in one's theoretical orientation. One scholar can place psychological factors at the center of his framework, whereas another may emphasize social conditions. For this reason, systematic study also calls for a coherent presentation of the intellectual assumptions underlying a body of research. Another way to avoid subjectivity is to check and recheck one's facts and conclusions with other students. This is why scholars write and publish their findings: so that their colleagues may read of their research and compare it with their own experience. Furthermore, those colleagues will be quick to reveal the assumptions that underlie a study; and they will point to factors that have been omitted and to others that have been given an exaggerated significance. All science, then, is "social" in that scientific truth requires the reaching of some agreement among the community of scholars who comprise a profession. On some questions, of course, there will never be agreement. For in many instances, the same set of facts can impel different conclusions from different observers; thus for all their attempts at consensus, students may still disagree over basic explanations of political behavior. Still, the aim of systematic study is to enlarge the area of agreed-upon knowledge and to reduce the realm of controversy.

POLITICAL PHILOSOPHY

Not all students of politics confine themselves to the quest for factual knowledge. Others are concerned with the search for *moral* knowledge. These political philosophers are interested not so much in how people and governments behave as they are in how they ought to behave. If the political scientist studies reality and tries to explain its functioning, the political philosopher studies ideas and tries to discover which have the greatest moral validity.

"THE GREAT BOOKS" Most of the great political philosophers are long since dead. The first great political thinker was Plato, who died in 347 B.C.

Since his time there have been no more than 20 or 25 writers whose ideas have endured through history. Yet the books that flowed from the pens of these authors can provide a lifetime's reading for the student of political philosophy. Plato's *Republic,* for example, is only several hundred pages long. It is a depiction of an imaginary society, a utopia, organized in such a way that the ideal of justice is made actual. In this book Plato constructs a philosophy of human nature, social structure, and the good life. The *Republic* is a book to be argued with, and men have been doing just that for well over a thousand years. One question is whether or not Plato's utopia is a totalitarian society, where human liberty is denied and authority exalted. To discuss such a problem it is necessary to read and reread the *Republic* with great care, asking what it was the author meant to say and why he framed his argument as he did. An understanding of Plato and the other great writers is fundamental to the study of political philosophy.

This is because the works of Plato—and of Aristotle, St. Thomas Aquinas, Niccolo Machiavelli, Thomas Hobbes, John Locke, Jean-Jacques Rousseau, Edmund Burke, Jeremy Bentham, Hegel, Karl Marx, and John Stuart Mill—all deal with the perennial questions of politics. They asked such questions as:

> What is justice?
> When should citizens obey the state?
> Are men equal?
> What makes authority legitimate?
> What is freedom?
> Is man good or evil?
> Is self-government possible?
> Are there laws of history?
> Which is prior: society or the individual?

These are moral questions, and there is more than one answer to each of them. Rousseau says that men are equal, and Burke would deny that proposition. Hegel asserts that society is more important than the individual, and Mill replies that the individual has priority over society.

The "great books," therefore, provide the best starting point for the study of the moral aspects of political life. The works of these authors endure because they dealt with fundamental questions, with problems that persist over time and that cross national boundaries. Not every generation or even every century produces a writer of the intellectual power of a Thomas Hobbes or a Jean-Jacques Rousseau. Indeed, we cannot say for sure if there are writers of their stature living among us right now. For it takes the passage of years, the test of time, before we know whether a political philosophy is destined to be of lasting value.

PHILOSOPHY OR OPINION?   Political philosophy must attempt to rise above ideology. Thus, for example, Americans who believe that the United States provides greater guarantees of liberty and justice for its citizens than do any other of the world's nations, should be obliged to show that they have studied other countries and have found them inferior to America after measuring them by some philosophic standard. For generalizations about how men and governments ought to behave should be framed in terms of enduring principles. This, for example, is what St. Thomas Aquinas had in mind when he spoke of the existence of a Natural Law. This body of precepts prescribes proper behavior at all times and in all places. But it is not a rigid doctrine, nor is it based on the experience of a single country. The Natural Law, St. Thomas points out, does not necessarily affirm the right to private property. This right, he says, should only be guaranteed if the principle of individual ownership fits in harmoniously with the general pattern of life of a society. Philosophy, then, deals with principles of political conduct. The pitfall to be avoided is that of attempting to defend one's own personal or national interests on philosophic grounds. To do that is to elevate personal opinions to an unwarranted height; it is, indeed, to indulge in ideology. Political philosophy, like political science, demands a detached and objective attitude of mind. None of us can be completely objective, but it is a goal we must strive for as best we can.

INSTITUTIONS AND BEHAVIOR

Most students of politics, most of the time, study the actual operations of governments. Scientific methods may be used in such study, and philosophical principles may underlie evaluations and analysis. But one recurrent focus of politics is on the workings of contemporary institutions.

What is an "institution"? Very simply, it is a group of people working toward a common aim. Thus a political party, a judicial tribunal, a legislative body, an administrative bureau—all these are institutions. The people who comprise them may come and go as time passes. Thus, leaders of the Republican party will rise and fall over a period of years but the party continues as an institution. Moreover, the common aim that an institution pursues can be a very general one. The members of Congress, for example, will not always agree on which bills should be passed or in what form. Nor will the judges of the Supreme Court always hand down unanimous decisions. But they do agree on when to meet, on how to handle their business, and on what it is they are supposed to be doing. Thus all congressmen know they are in Washington to pass laws; all justices know it is their job to decide cases. An institution, then, consists of individuals, general goals, and rules for reaching those goals. There can be a one-man institution such as the Presidency; or a multimillion-member institution such as a political party. Some institutions have limited goals and others have more comprehensive programs. In some the members are strong in their loyalty to the group's aims; in others they are apathetic or even obstructive. It remains to say that politics cannot function without institutions, and an understanding of politics requires an awareness of how they operate.

HOW GOVERNMENT OPERATES   The student of institutions wants to find out how men organize themselves to secure ends they think desirable. In the context of American government such an undertaking might inquire:

> How are individual freedoms guaranteed?
> Where does the sovereign power reside?
> How do citizens select their rulers?
> Who makes the laws?
> How are laws administered and enforced?
> What is the proper role of government?

These questions, needless to say, are highly theoretical; and any attempt to discuss them in generalized terms will probably end in frustration. What is needed is an understanding of specific institutions and their operation. Some of these institutions might be:

> The writ of certiorari
> The Tenth Amendment to the Constitution
> Party primaries and nominating conventions

> The Rules Committee of the House of Representatives
> The Office of Management and Budget
> The Tennessee Valley Authority

Thus, the Supreme Court plays a vital role in deciding which liberties are to be guaranteed to citizens. The Court will hear a case if four justices indicate, through a writ of certiorari, that' they think such a hearing is warranted. The writ itself may be no more than a piece of paper, but it is the Supreme Court acting as an institution that uses the rule to protect the freedoms of individuals. By the same token the Court employs the Tenth Amendment, another rule on paper, to decide which are the sovereign powers of the several states and which powers belong properly to the federal government. Thus, freedoms are defined and sovereignty is located through institutional means. Meaningful answers to theoretical questions are given in the decisions of our highest judicial institution.

If it is asked how citizens select the men and women who are to hold public office, a large part of the answer lies in the process whereby candidates are nominated. Hence, it is necessary to know who participates in the primaries and who attends the nominating conventions— and how these institutions work. Moreover, some study must be given to the reasons why people participate in party politics and why they vote as they do. Where, for example, do citizens get their political values? How do they express their values through voting? Quite clearly such study must be "scientific" in the sense that the behavior of voters must be examined in a systematic way.

While it is obvious that our elected lawmakers make our laws, it is also true that in the Congress there are centers of power having disproportionate control over the legislative process. Here an institution like the Rules Committee of the House of Representatives will play a crucial role. For despite the fact that all congressmen have one vote, there is nevertheless a complex network of agencies within the Congress deciding which issues will ultimately become law of the land.

The executive power is vested in the President, but the Constitution spells out this power in only the most rudimentary way. If he has the responsibility of administering and enforcing the laws, he must find institutional means for doing the job at hand. Over the years, therefore, the Presidency has evolved methods for coordinating the activities of its administration. An important institution is the Office of Management and Budget, a body reporting directly to the White House and one that helps the President to control the multifarious functions of the executive branch. While presidential power depends in large measure on the temperament of the Chief Executive and the temper of the times, its day-to-day operations rely heavily on institutions like the Office of Management and Budget.

To ask what is the proper role of government in American society is to pose a philosophical question. But before one starts developing one's own ideas on the matter, it is worth giving some attention to the functions that government currently performs. The Tennessee Valley Authority, for example, is an institution owned and operated by the federal government; and, among other things, it is in the business of producing and selling electric power. Why is the government in this business at all? How efficient is the TVA operation? Before commencing on philosophical speculation it is advisable to examine the institutions upon which judgment is to be passed.

POLITICAL BEHAVIOR By this time it should be apparent that political institutions cannot be assumed to operate according to printed rule or to adhere to the lines laid out on organization charts. Thus, for example, Executive departments that desire new legislation are supposed to gain approval for those requests from the Office of Management and Budget before an approach is made to the Congress. Such clearance ensures that administration policy follows a consistent pattern and that different bureaus are not working at cross-purposes. However, in practice, a whole network of informal relationships has grown up between veteran civil servants and influential congressmen, bypassing the Office of Management and Budget, and resulting in acts or appropriations the President may consider unnecessary or even harmful. Behavior of this sort must be acknowledged and understood if institutions are to be realistically depicted. Moreover, the individuals involved give shape to institutional operations. Whether the office is the director of the Federal Bureau of Investigation, majority leader of the Senate, or Chief Justice of the United States, the attitudes and outlook of the person holding those positions will influence its policies and posture.

In addition, not all political activity occurs in institutional settings. A group of citizens who gather one evening in the street to protest against some intrusion in their neighborhood do not comprise an "institution." Nor do the processes by which policies are decided always adhere to institutional channels. Consumer boycotts, student protests, and even prison riots can all stir lawmakers and administrators to action. Put another way, alongside the country's institutional structures, there exist millions of daily actions that make up the parameters of politics. These even include the unseen process whereby an average citizen slowly begins to change his mind as he absorbs new information about a political issue.

The study of political behavior—sometimes called the "behavioral approach" to politics—relies on a wide variety of methods and disciplines, if only because its subject matter is so extensive. These can include sample surveys, of the sort described earlier in this chapter, which attempt to find out why citizens behave as they do. Other methods involve the use of mathematical models, aiming at discovering the roles played by different variables in a given situation. Such a model might seek to simulate the way in which this country conducts its international relations, by hypothesizing alternating combinations of factors that contribute to the making of foreign policy. Another behavioral approach will focus on devising a general theory of human interaction, starting with the premise that the political process is an ongoing "system" and then trying to work out the parts played by diverse determinants in that environment. Thus, for example, the phenomenon of urban crime may be seen not simply as lawbreaking, but as forms of behavior serving important functions in the light of prevailing economic, ethnic, and cultural conditions. In these and other instances, the emphasis is on systematic observation, calling for the creation of reliable data and its analysis in the context of theoretical frameworks. Behavior can be construed as individual or institutional; in fact, it involves a series of subtle relationships between actual people and the structures they use to achieve ends of their choosing.

HOW TO STUDY A POLITICAL PROBLEM Government is a highly complex operation, and patterns of political behavior are highly variable. On some occasions it is possible to generalize, on others it is not and one must settle for an understanding of how different institutions operate in their own setting. For example, sometimes it is appropriate to make a general statement about the workings of all American legislative chambers. But on certain matters it is necessary to distinguish between the Senate, the House of Representatives, and the state legislatures. A good rule of thumb is that whenever possible one should work from the particular to the general, drawing detailed information together and framing conclusions of ever-widening applicability.

If the goal of political study is the creation of valid generalizations, the path to this goal is not as smooth as might first appear. Ideological overtones are apt to infuse any attempt at either "scientific" or "philosophical" conclusions, and these intrusions must be guarded against. The student must seek an awareness of his personal values and must sense when they are prejudicing his analysis. He must also be willing to compare his findings and conclusions with those of others, for only out of such a community of knowledge does the whole truth emerge. If facts are to be used to support a conclusion, then they must be gathered and organized according to a system: methods of analysis and inquiry must be easily described and made available to anyone who wishes to duplicate one's research so as to test its validity. Finally, there are considerations of values in all political study and these values lie at the foundation of political life. There is no significance in simply describing an institution of government as an end in itself. Citizens engage in politics to achieve purposes they think right, and by the same token the student must frame his researches in a philosophical context. He, too, must ask what are the aims and ends of governmental activity. And he must be prepared to evaluate that activity on the basis of principles which he has not only selected for himself but which he must be able to defend.

The study of politics, then, consists of weaving together a cloth of many fabrics. Political science and political philosophy must be synthesized in a coherent way; political institutions and political behavior must be viewed in a framework of interaction; political ideology and political principle must be described and differentiated. The final arrangement of these various approaches is the task of each person who elects to observe and comment upon the political scene. For it is his imagination, coupled with his intelligence and his powers of perception, that must make ultimate sense out of that omnipresent phenomenon we call the political life.

REVIEW QUESTIONS

1. Does democracy postulate that all political opinions are equal?

2. What is ideology?

3. How does political science differ from the natural and physical sciences? In what ways is it similar?

4. Why do students of politics find value in Plato's *Republic?*

5. How does a political philosophy differ from a personal opinion?

6. What is an institution?

2 MAN AND SOCIETY

The drama of politics is played on the stage we call society. And its cast of characters consists of men and women of varying backgrounds, interests, and temperaments. Political life can be understood only if it is seen in its social setting and viewed in terms of the human beings who give it substance. Theories of politics, therefore, must be underpinned by theories of man and society.

HUMAN NATURE

The question—What is Man?—has been asked for thousands of years and has yet to receive a satisfying answer. For neither professional philosophers nor amateur observers have been able to agree on the essential characteristics of human nature. Although everyone has had

17

experience of life among his fellow men and women, each person has his own perception of himself and those around him. In consequence, a whole multitude of theories have developed, no one of which is wholly true but none of which can be proven to be altogether false. Still, it is possible to stand aside and analyze these contrasting perceptions of man. And, in the course of doing so, a student may find himself concluding that the truth lies somewhat closer to one view than to another.

GOOD OR EVIL?   "That men are actually wicked, a sad and continued experience of them proves beyond doubt," Jean-Jacques Rousseau wrote. "But all the same, I think I have shown that man is naturally good." According to this view all men are born into the world in a state of natural goodness. They are benign creatures, endowed with the potentiality for harmonious life with their fellows. Thus the traits of altruism, congeniality, and compassion are seen as being innate in the human species. If men and women are regarded as isolated individuals there is much evidence to support the theory of natural goodness. Apart from occasional misanthropes, it is clear that human beings are capable of expressing kindness and generosity. Even those who appear to be cynical and callous in their dealings with others can be shown to have a warmer side to their nature. The heart of gold beneath the jaded exterior is, of course, a cliché of countless movie scripts, television programs, and magazine stories. It is interesting to note that so many of us *want* to believe that man is good.

But the modern world is no paradise. Indeed, since the beginning of history societies and nations have been blemished by war, injustice, and tyranny. If man is naturally good, then how can these evils be explained? The usual response is to begin by assuming that while man himself possesses and has always possessed the ability to live in peace and freedom, when men act perversely it is because they have been corrupted by the institutions of society. For no theory proposes that "society" is naturally good. There are all kinds of societies and social institutions, some of which bring out the best in man and others that degrade him. Thus, if men exhibit selfish behavior it is because they live in a society that compels or rewards such attributes. Some writers claim that the institution of private property makes men materialistic and causes them to promote their own interests to the detriment of others. Other thinkers may feel that the expansion of governmental power prevents individuals from developing their true capabilities. But in both cases the men and women who make up society are not to be blamed for acting as they do. The responsibility must be attributed to the rise of identifiable institutions that cramp and corrupt the natural goodness that is waiting to be released if only given the chance.

ORIGINAL SIN "History," Edmund Burke concluded, "consists for the greater part of the miseries brought upon the world by pride, ambition, avarice, revenge, lust, sedition, hypocrisy, ungoverned zeal, and all the traits of disorderly appetites which shake the public." Not only is this the history of the human condition as it has been in the past; it is also a description of human nature as it always will be. Pride, ambition, avarice—all these characteristics and more, it is suggested, are sewn into the nature of man. Individuals may display an altruistic side from time to time; but it is a mistake to assume that men are for that reason naturally good. On the contrary, the evidence of history is that people are usually concerned with their own welfare first and foremost. If men are claimed to harbor the potentiality for living in peace and harmony, it may therefore be asked how it is that this potentiality has not yet been realized in our several thousand years of political life? Indeed the world's recent experience of tyranny and injustice indicates that men are as evil in our time as they have ever been in the past. Probably more so.

The doctrine of original sin postulates that human nature is unchanging and unchangeable. Since Adam's act of disobedience, this theory proceeds, all men have been tainted by his transgression. Each individual born onto this earth is a fallible creature, and during his lifetime he will act in perverse ways. Everyone without exception exhibits these failings, and all societies everywhere inevitably contain at least some members who undermine efforts to create social harmony. According to this view, institutions are not the molders of character but rather reflections of human nature. If there are inequalities of wealth or power, these stem from the self-interest that is built into social behavior. Any attempt to make over the basic structure of society, moreover, will be as unsuccessful as would an attempt to alter human character. This is because both men and societies are the products of a history they did not themselves make. Indeed, such social and political reforms as are effected will seldom bring the blessings that the reformers originally intended. For human perversity cannot be abolished by plans or programs. The best that can be done is to control the worst manifestations of this perversity by means of political authority: police, civil penalties, or the threat of imprisonment. If freedom and justice are to have any meaning, they must be guaranteed by governmental sanctions. "Society," Burke continued, "requires not only that the passions of individuals should be subjected, but that even in the mass and body, as well as in the individuals, the inclinations of men should frequently be thwarted, their will controlled, and their passions brought into subjection."

RATIONAL OR IRRATIONAL? "Why is it," John Stuart Mill asked, "that there is on the whole a preponderance among mankind of rational opinions and rational conduct?" The answer Mill gives is straightforward. To begin with, if man were not rational—that is, unable to select means to achieve the ends he desires—then the business of politics and society would deteriorate into chaos. History does show that men have been able, by the use of reason, to devise ways of splitting the atom, delivering the mail, and even on occasion of preventing wars. Rationality is possible because man is a creature who has shown himself capable of learning by experience. His knowledge is cumulative and he can forbear from repeating the mistakes of the past. This, at least, is one view of human nature. The question of whether man is fundamentally rational or irrational is different from but related to the question of whether he is basically good or evil. Men can be good but also irrational; they can be evil but nevertheless rational. One question deals with the shape of the human spirit; the other with the powers of the human mind.

It can be argued that just as men are good when approached as isolated individuals, so are they rational when they consider the affairs in the solitude of their own home. However, once men are brought together in crowds they tend to lose their heads. They can be stirred by demagogues and lured into supporting policies and programs that they would reject in a saner moment. Thus apparently rational individuals will become transformed as they join a lynch mob or a revolutionary movement. So will hitherto sensible citizens express support for expensive programs (such as "massive rehabilitation of the slums") but then not provide the money or pay for them or the personnel to implement them. The conclusion emerges that if men as individuals are rational, society as an entity is often lacking this quality.

Juxtaposed against this view is an altogether different theory. Here it is proposed that men are irrational, that they are creatures of passion and interest. "Thus the passions of men are gratified," Hegel wrote. "They develop themselves and their aims in accordance with their natural tendencies, and build up the edifice of human society. . . . In history an additional result is commonly produced by human actions beyond that which they aim at and obtain." The thought is that history has a rationality of its own, a logic that unfolds independent of the behavior of individuals. Thus, as thousands or millions of men and women strive to gratify their passions or promote their interests, there come into being consequences that they did not anticipate and that they cannot prevent. The course of history, then, is unrelenting and is guided by a "reason" unique to itself. The best that men can hope for is to *understand* the underlying forces that move nations and societies. According to this view, knowledge rather than action should be the goal. For at least it can be said that men who understand the reason of history will not be surprised or bewildered as the future unfolds around them.

SUPERIOR PEOPLE AND INFERIOR PEOPLE   For better or for worse, we tend to remark on the factors that distinguish one person from another rather than the characteristics all people have in common. How much can we say (or do we wish to say) about the qualities held alike by poets and day laborers, by physicists and petty thieves? While everyone is "human," and presumably entitled to dignity and respect, the impetus to grade individuals still emerges in most societies. The whole question of human equality will be considered more fully in later chapters. What requires analysis at this point are the criteria that have been used for differentiating members of a political population. In particular, if a society contains individuals of "superior" caliber, we should make clear what separates them from their less-blessed fellow citizens.

1. The first conception of superiority ascribes special qualities to people born into a certain grouping. Thus it may be argued that women are more imaginative than men, or that Orientals evidence higher intelligence than individuals having other colorations. Hence the argument that there are "superior races" or that some strains of humanity carry genes of a higher endowment. Anyone who believes this must be prepared to answer several critical questions. Suppose it can be shown, for example, that Americans of Japanese descent, taken together, score

higher on intelligence tests than do citizens of Norwegian origin. This may indeed be true. (We know that as a group, women get higher grades in liberal arts subjects than do men.) But are these sufficient data on which to make generalizations? For there will invariably be some Norwegian-Americans who score better than at least some of the Japanese-Americans. Therefore it cannot be asserted that everyone having Japanese ancestry has a better mind than every person with Norwegian antecedents. And if such a general statement cannot be made, it is best to refrain from statements suggesting the innate superiority of individuals having particular lineages or physiologies. In other words, averages and composites do not account for the exceptions. And so long as exceptions exist, a special "nature" should not be ascribed to all members of an entire group. (Moreover, intelligence tests measure only a single quality: one's ability to do well on intelligence tests.)

2. A second conception of superiority focuses on circumstances of birth as well, but here attention is drawn to men and women who happen to possess inherited wealth, privileged education, and who are members of families that have exercised power and responsibility for at least several generations. What makes these people "superior"? The argument is sometimes made that "blood tells," that genetic inheritance produces superior qualities in certain family lines. However, this theory is questionable, if only because even the best families have their share of idiots and immoralists. Rather the case rests on the view that those who are brought up in an atmosphere of inherited wealth develop a sense of security and self-confidence that is usually denied to others. This class has both the education and the leisure to evolve a style of life that raises the level of culture and civility in society. Having roots in their civilization's tradition and being able to take a long-range perspective on the future, their approach to politics is conservative in the best sense. And because members of this class have material security, they often enter civic or political life out of a sense of duty. This means they can promote the broader interests of society and do not have to pander to the momentary whims of a capricious electorate. A man of wealth does not have to build a political career in order to feed his family. He can be available when he is needed; but he can also resign when he feels his principles are being compromised. To be sure, not all individuals in this class display this sense of responsibility. There is no shortage of playboys among the old rich. But what is argued is that an aristocracy of

breeding does, on the whole, promote the higher values and the finer things of life. Although this class may live off the sweat of others, the culture that it sustains raises the quality of life for everyone. Whether it be art or literature or constitutional liberty, the suggestion is that these values are supported by a minority of wealth, education, and leisure. And all society profits because such standards are strengthened and transmitted.

3. At the same time, experience has shown that many of our finest intellects spring from humble surroundings. What is pointed out is that there are some people, regardless of origin, who possess extraordinary minds. These individuals have powers of perception usually denied to others; they can detect an order in human affairs and can discern major trends that are obscure to the generality of their fellow citizens. Most members of this group of superior people have little contact with the enterprise of politics; they are artists or writers or teachers, or are similarly removed from circles where power is exercised. However, some theorists have concluded that the good society will be attained only if philosophers become kings. Yet seldom throughout history have men and women of superior intellect been placed in positions where they may have an impact on the conduct of government. Thus the question is whether these people should play a greater role in politics, especially at the higher reaches where policies having far-reaching implications are made.

Moreover, it is sometimes suggested that among this "aristocracy of intellect" there are persons of superior *moral* knowledge. Here are individuals who can rise above emotions and interests, and who can see the meaning of justice and virtue in ways that others cannot. Such men of reason can detect the common good or the general welfare while others think only of self-interest. In this sense the possession of rationality means not only being able to perceive the world as it is, but also being able to judge how the world ought to be. The argument therefore is that wisdom must be joined by virtue, that citizens who possess these qualities should be elevated to positions of power and influence. To be sure, there is bound to be controversy over what is virtue or what is the common good. But few will deny that it is better to have men of moral sensibility in government than men who think only of power and profit.

4. One of the reasons why persons of superior breeding and intellect are not so prominent as they might be in political life is that they are

frequently overshadowed by another group. For there is also in every society a series of individuals who have an aptitude for exercising power. This ability to influence others is sometimes found in those of privileged background, for they have the self-confidence that imparts the authority to command. And it occasionally occurs in individuals with superior intellects, because they can discern the symbols and techniques that make men obey. But on the whole, the talents of power bear little relation to family background or high intelligence. At the head of armies and of mobs, of business enterprises and government bureaucracies, indeed in all situations where men work and act together, will be found talented individuals who know how to lead others.

Such extraordinary individuals may spend little time considering questions of culture or morality. They are more expert in manipulating means than they are in pondering ends. Many of them have devoted time and energy to building their careers and they often think more of their own prospects than they do of the common good. Moreover, the talents of leadership are governed by the time, the place, and the circumstances. A man may show great abilities for leading a revolutionary movement and if he is available at the right juncture he will be able to exercise his superior talents. However, another epoch in history may call for someone to oversee a complex bureaucracy, and here will be needed an individual who can administer intricate policies and lead an organization. In other words, the talent for haranguing a mob is quite different from the talent of heading a civil service. Yet both are talents and both are talents of leadership. At the same time, the ability to lead leaves open the question of the goals that are being pursued. Quite clearly, most successful leaders are not philosophers and many promote the interests of a group or a class rather than that of society as a whole. But talent cannot be submerged for long, and men able to exercise power will usually find an outlet for their calling.

Any theory of human nature, therefore, must take account of the characteristics that differentiate individuals from each other. Men may be good or evil or a mixture of the two. They may be rational or irrational or both. But there is always the suspicion that there are some people who are exceptions to any generalizations about human nature. Whether it is legitimate to talk of such persons as "extraordinary" at all is a recurrent question of political theory. It may be that superior breeding or intellect or talent sets particular individuals apart from the rest of their fellow men and women. Or it may be that despite their superiority in some respects they are, in essentials, pretty much like the rest of us.

THE STRUCTURE OF SOCIETY

Theories of society can either attempt to describe the structure of society as it actually is or they can propose ways in which it should be organized. However, this simple distinction between "scientific" theories on the one hand, and "philosophical" theories on the other, is seldom manifested in political writings. What usually happens is that a theorist begins with his own conception of the *good* society. It may well be that he prefers arrangements pretty much as they are. If this is the case, then his "scientific" description of reality will actually highlight the more praiseworthy aspects of the status quo and will tend to overlook those that are more depressing. Another theorist may be upset by things as they are, and for him the good society will be radically different from what he sees about him. In this instance, his "scientific" description will emphasize the unsavory conditions of the present system. This needs to be said because every theory of society is necessarily colored by the moral preconceptions of its author. The observer, in the final analysis, sees the society he *wants* to see. The value of a theory lies in its ability to convince others that its depiction of reality is consistent with their own experience of life in this world. It is not surprising, therefore, that there are two quite different and opposing views of society in political theory. These may be called the "atomistic" view and the "organic" view.

THE ATOMISTIC VIEW "The community is a fictitious body," Jeremy Bentham wrote, "composed of the individual persons who are considered as constituting as it were its members." When someone calls community or society a "fiction," his intention is to stress the fact that these entities are no more than collections of individual citizens. This atomistic view asserts that any social whole is simply the sum of its individual parts. To claim that a community or a society is somehow greater than or independent of the people who compose it is a risky enterprise. For then one is tempted to say that society has a "life" or a "purpose" or even a "destiny" of its own, and such an assertion is pure conjecture. At all events, the atomistic approach assumes that a society and its component institutions are brought into being by men for reasons of necessity or convenience. A number of theorists have argued, for example, that at some time in the past citizens came out of the primeval forest ("the state of nature") and formally agreed to set up society and government ("the social contract") as a means of solving the problems of anarchy and injustice. Although the ideas of a "state of nature" and a "social contract" are themselves fictions, they serve to emphasize the point that society exists for the benefit of its citizens.

This also means that social and political institutions—churches, schools, businesses, associations, courts, legislatures—must give evidence that they exist to further the welfare of the people who either belong to them or who must submit to their authority. The atomistic theory implies that there should be a minimum of barriers to the development of individual potentialities. Society must serve the needs of citizens and encourage them to evolve their best qualities. For this reason social and political power should be fragmented rather than concentrated. Whether the power of government or any other institution is being considered, the suspicion remains that any concentration of power deters individuals from expressing themselves to the foremost of their capabilities. For a surfeit of restrictions dampens the human spirit and destroys initiative. It is not surprising, therefore, that the atomistic view often postulates an elemental conflict between "man and the state" or between "authority and the individual." Such tensions can indeed exist, and the atomistic prescription is that they should be resolved in favor of the citizen rather than the state or society. The answer is less clear-cut, of course, when there are conflicts between citizen and citizen. And there are also cases of discord between a majority of citizens on the one hand and a minority on the other. Both majority and minority are collections of individuals, and principles and procedures must be devised for settling the differences of opinion and interest that inevitably occur.

ATOMISM AND PLURALISM   At the same time, no society is an undifferentiated mass of individuals. Every society has a "structure," and in the atomistic view this structure is a network of groups and associations. People in a society may be distinguished from each other on the basis of race or religion or national origin. They will live in different regions of the country and hence have different habits and patterns of thought. Thus there will be Protestants and Roman Catholics, Italian-Americans and Anglo-Saxons, New Yorkers and Californians, and so forth. Some of these group memberships or identifications will change as individuals shift their residence or enter into new strata of the society. What is being stressed, however, is that there is a diversity of groups and that these groups interact with each other in much the same way that individuals do among themselves. At the same time citizens are free to part company with one or another group when such an identification ceases to prove advantageous to them. There is nothing in the atomistic theory that says that a person must remain a Presbyterian or a Pennsylvanian if he finds such a role constricting. To be sure, a person cannot throw off his racial background. But he can, if he works at it, go a long way toward severing his ties with a group that no longer gives him the opportunities he wants.

By the same token, an atomistic society is a "nation of joiners." There are many associations ranging from garden clubs to political parties, from civic welfare organizations to lobbies and pressure groups. The assumption is that people join these associations voluntarily with a variety of motives. It is further supposed that most people are "joiners" and are prepared to promote their interests by combining with others who have similar views. The motive may be simply to have fun: such as forming a ski club or a bowling league. Or it may be economic and political: as joining together to petition the legislature to pass a law that will benefit a neighborhood or an industry. The fact that society contains many associations has a number of consequences. For one thing, it takes individuals out of a state of isolation and gives them a chance to participate with others in a common endeavor. For another, it permits citizens to have a variety of loyalties and allegiances, thus preventing the possibility that they might live under a single source of authority. Finally, a network of voluntary associations stands as a "buffer" between the relatively powerless individual and the potentially powerful state. In a way, association membership can act as a "shield" that protects a person from victimization at the hands of the agencies of government. Pluralism, therefore, is a natural accompaniment of the atomistic views of society and human freedom. The atomistic society, far from consisting of a mass of isolated individuals, is actually a web of associations and groups that link men and women with each other.

THE ORGANIC VIEW "Because it is the completion of associations existing by nature," Aristotle wrote, "every *polis* [i.e., society] exists by nature, having itself the same quality as the earlier associations from which it grew." This conception looks on society as a natural phenomenon, having grown out of the family, the clan, and more primitive forms of collective life. To regard society as an "organism" is to see it as a series of enduring relationships between people and institutions. That is, each citizen and association has a place and function in the social whole, and it is the obligation of each to contribute to the life and purpose of the community. Thus society at any point in time is the most recent culmination of a long natural and historical development. Rather than being a contract of convenience made by men and capable of being broken by them, it is a living organism with a past and a future. Moreover, in the organic view a society is a genuine community; citizens have a sense of belonging and they receive their values and their identity from participation in communal life.

This society is also pluralistic, but it is a different kind of pluralism. There will be a variety of groups and associations; however, they will not move around aimlessly like so many atoms. On the contrary, churches and civic organizations and fraternal groups will have a location in the social structure established by history and tradition. Indeed, the entire structure of the organic society is characterized by a hierarchy. There will be various classes of citizens existing in a pyramidal order and each class will have its own rights and responsibilities. Thus, while the members of the upper class may have inherited wealth and power, they will also assume the duty of acting in the best interests of those arrayed beneath them in the social order. Out of this arrangement there emerges a dependence of all groups and classes upon one another. For the rich need the poor just as the poor need the rich. The relationship is not one of exploitation, but rather of mutual acknowledgment that each part of the community has a role to play in the pursuit of the common good.

COMMUNITY AND INDIVIDUALITY The organic society cannot permit too much mobility on the part of individuals. For the happiness of the citizens and the welfare of the community, it is best that most persons remain throughout their lives in the regions and classes in which they were born. Most renderings of the organic outlook are essentially conservative in that they carry the implicit assumption that individuals will feel confident in their values and that society will remain stable only if everyone accepts his traditional role and carries it out to the best of his ability. Even the most humble of occupations has a dignity of its own, and the rubrics of "success" and "failure" have no meaning in an organic setting. Each citizen, and not simply those at the summit of the social pyramid, profits from remaining in his established station. For by doing so he finds human relationships predictable and he can be sure that the values of his forebears are applicable to life as he knows it. While the atomistic theory stresses individualism, its organic counterpart underlines the security and contentment produced by living in a community where each citizen is respected for the part he takes in promoting the welfare of all. Individual happiness, then, stands in an integral relationship to the stability and health of the entire society. Progress is a slow historical process and the institutions of social life are the results of a natural evolution. Attempts to hasten or upset this development by artificial means will end in chaos, for the fabric of an organic society is woven in a complex pattern that is easily torn but virtually impossible to repair.

ATOMISTIC OR ORGANIC? Two questions must be asked in the course of evaluating any theory. The first is: Does the theory give a satisfactory description of social and political life as it actually *is*? The second is: Does it provide a persuasive prescription for the kind of society and political system that *ought* to exist? Both of these questions are relevant to the atomistic and organic theories; for both deal with description and prescription, with the "is" and the "ought."

Most commentators will agree that, in general outlines, modern societies are more atomistic than organic. They argue that industrialization and urbanization have liberated individuals from the fixed roles and relationships of an earlier time. The organic theory may have been an adequate description of agrarian society of the feudal or preindustrial epoch. Institutions today take on more of the fluid character of voluntary associations than they do the established patterns of medieval guilds. The organic theorist does not deny the advent of industrialization, nor does he ignore the fact that mobility has become accelerated in recent generations. What he argues is that society ought to understand that the appearance of progress can in fact be retrogression. Many trends, such as the rapid growth of indust ν and the displacement of individuals from classes and callings in which they were reared, are actually harmful to the proper functioning of the organism. Human freedom, in this view, has been expanding too rapidly for its own good. Moreover, its movements have been in the wrong direction, for they tend to deprive men of the moral values and sense of security they need to lead the full life.

Thus the question becomes a moral one. The defender of the atomistic view claims that his kind of society liberates men, that it releases them from feudal bonds and allows them to develop their full potentialities as individuals. The proponent of the organic view counters that there is such a thing as having too much freedom, that individuals can lead the good life only if they receive from society an authoritative set of values. In a sense, the question revolves around how much freedom men want or need, and how this freedom is to be defined. It is also a question concerning the definition of human nature, for until one has a clear conception of man's capabilities, it is impossible to know what kind of society he must have if he is to experience freedom and happiness.

REVIEW QUESTIONS

1. What does it mean to say that "man is naturally good"?
2. In what senses can some men be said to be superior to others?
3. What is a "social contract"?
4. What is pluralism?
5. How can society be an organism?
6. Is progress always desirable?

3 ENDS AND MEANS

The great issues of political theory have been defined and debated for more than 2,000 years. The vocabulary of political theory, unlike that of many other disciplines, is a part of the public domain. Thus, everyone is prepared to discourse on liberty and equality, on law and justice, on power and policy. Indeed, there are many people who feel that they have their own "theories" on these subjects. But not all attempts to generalize about political life are worthy of being called theoretical. A theory must be clear and consistent, it must be grounded on a sophisticated awareness of the facts, it must not be distorted by emotions or interests. This does not mean that two theories cannot reach opposed conclusions.

Indeed, this is just what occurred in the case of theories about society. The best way to discuss this question is to turn to some actual theories dealing with significant political issues.

TWO THEORIES OF FREEDOM

FREEDOM FROM RESTRAINT "By liberty, is understood, according to the proper signification of the word, the absence of external impediments," Thomas Hobbes wrote. A free man, according to this theory, is one who is not prevented from doing the things he wants to do. Men seek to express themselves in a wide variety of ways. Some put a high premium on practicing their religion and worshiping God as their conscience dictates. Others like to make speeches or write books. Still others desire to form political parties or social movements. And yet another group wishes to run their own businesses and enrich themselves in the process. To be able to do any or all of these things is to be free. To want to do them, but to be barred from doing so, is to be subjected to oppression. The quest for freedom, then, involves removing the barriers to individual action. It also involves preventing the raising of new barriers. The old dictum is also a true one: Eternal vigilance is the price of liberty. The problem for some men is keeping the freedoms they have. The problem for others is securing the freedoms they want but do not have. Needless to say, in many instances a victory on the part of the "have-nots" may result in diminishing the freedoms of the "haves."

FREEDOM AND GOVERNMENT What are the barriers to individual freedom? Some theorists regard the government as the foremost threat to individual liberty. There is more than enough evidence in history to show that governments have proscribed religions, banned books, abolished parties, and confiscated property. It is not surprising that governments have been able to do this, for the state has at its disposal the power to make and enforce laws, and it has in its service the police and the army. A free society, in this view, is one in which the powers of government are severely limited in scope. The customary proposal is that the functions of government be outlined in a constitution, which specifies what kinds of official sanctions are permitted and which are prohibited. In this way, citizens have a defined area of freedom, where they may express themselves without encountering governmental regulation or interference. Needless to say, a constitutional document cannot in itself assure political freedom. A society must also seek to develop a tradition and atmosphere of tolerance if individual rights are to be guaranteed in practice as well as on paper. At the same time, people may more effectively question the actions of government if they can point to particular provisions which they feel official agencies have violated.

While government has the power to make laws and to coerce citizens, many writers and thinkers feel that impediments to freedom can spring from other sources in society. It is often argued that individuals are frustrated in their desires not so much by the state as by their fellow citizens. Neighbors may make life difficult for someone who tries to practice an unorthodox religion. A wealthy employer may, in various ways, deprive his employees of freedoms they believe they should have. In instances such as these, religious heretics or exploited employees may look to the government for protection. In other words, they hope that the force of governmental power will permit them the freedoms they did not previously have. According to this analysis, the government can be the guarantor of freedoms. The big question, therefore, is which class or group in society can dominate the governmental machinery or at least gain access to it. But whether the state is regarded as the enemy or friend of liberty the overarching view here is that freedom is something that the individual can define and evaluate for himself. The idea is that each citizen knows what it is he wants to do and he can tell whether or not he is being allowed to do it.

POSITIVE FREEDOM "He will be forced to be free," Jean-Jacques Rousseau wrote, "for this is the condition which, by giving each citizen to his country, secures him against all personal dependence." How can someone be "forced" to be free? By commonsense standards, freedom and compulsion are contradictory terms. However, here the answer is that genuine freedom consists in doing not simply what one wants to do, but rather in doing what one *ought* to do. Many human wants are little more than momentary whims. Gratifying these urges may be a kind of freedom, but it certainly is not a very elevated form. Everyone will admit that at one time or another he or she has acted "against his better judgment." However, that moment of recognition often comes too late in the day or even in life, and for some it never comes at all. Therefore, if people are to be truly free, they must be prevented from doing some of the things they want to do—or think they want to do. What is implied in this view, furthermore, is that society rather than the individual has the best understanding of what constitutes the free life. The history of one's nation and the customs of one's community have evolved values and standards by which freedom is defined. If a person is thrown on his own resources and tries to find a meaningful definition of freedom by himself, the odds are that he will fail in this endeavor. He is, in the final analysis, a citizen of his country and a member of his community, and true freedom for him is ultimately to be found in accepting the morality that has been prepared for him.

This, then, is why some dissentient citizens must be "forced" to be free. Put simply, they may think they know what they *want* in order to be free; but they are actually ignorant of the conditions they *need* to be truly free. Furthermore, once they have been compelled to take an alternative path, they will usually acknowledge that they had been wrong in their earlier judgment. The positive theory of freedom, therefore, is concerned with raising men to the level where they can best exercise whatever mental and moral faculties they have. The emphasis is on being free to do the things one ought to be doing. And it is the obligation of government to educate and elevate citizens in this positive direction.

The positive theory would appear to be saying that the average person is incapable of knowing his own best interests. Does this mean that every government should be headed by an elite that defines the meaning of freedom for everyone else? Some writers do suggest that rule by philosopher-kings is the only solution for the problem of freedom. However, most of them assume that the essential spirit of freedom is to be found in the history, the customs, and the traditions of a nation or a community. This means that attention must be paid to the lessons of the past and to the consensus that characterizes the present. Freedom is best viewed as the composite of freedoms that a society already possesses, the utility of which has been proven by time and experience. Does this mean, too, that the positive theory of freedom is fundamentally conservative? It is certainly true that it frequently accompanies the organic view of society and is used as an argument against social or political reform. But others than conservatives have taken the positive and organic approach. Karl Marx and Friedrich Engels wrote, "Only in community with others has each individual the means of cultivating his gifts in all directions; only in the community, therefore, is personal freedom possible." In other words, positive freedom can be a revolutionary as well as a conservative theory. For both revolutionaries and conservatives can be critical of the view of man and society that permits atomistic individuals to clash and compete with each other in their drive for wealth, status, and power.

FREEDOM OF THE WILL "The authority of a king is physical and controls the actions of men without subduing their will," Alexis de Tocqueville wrote. "But the majority possesses a power that is physical and moral at the same time, which acts upon the will as much as upon the actions." A tyrannical ruler may ban all opposition parties and jail or threaten those who criticize his regime. These restraints are oppressive to those who suffer them, but at least this use of power is visible to the eye. A man who has been imprisoned by a tyrant sees and feels his chains. But his mind remains free; if he is being oppressed, he *knows* he is being oppressed. However, there are other and more subtle forms of tyranny. A country may ostensibly be a democracy, where the majority has the power to rule. The individuals who comprise this majority may *think* they have power, may *think* they are free, and may *think* they have formed their ideas and opinions by themselves. Yet despite this apparently happy state of affairs, the fact may be that these citizens have had their attitudes and behavior shaped for them by the pressures to conformity exerted on them by society. Thus, freedom can be endangered by a tyranny that is invisible: the power a group exercises over the mentalities of its members. There are no prisons or chains, but rather the internalized attitudes that each person accepts and even welcomes. The curious question then arises: Can a man who thinks he is free actually be a slave? Put another way: Can we distinguish the "feeling of freedom" from "genuine freedom"? If such a distinction is valid, then it is necessary to give close attention to the forces that shape the minds of men. It is one thing to revolt against a visible tyrant. It is far more difficult to rebel against social pressures that cannot be seen.

EQUAL RIGHTS FOR EQUAL MEN
The discussion of theories of human nature brought out the fact that there are great differences in backgrounds and characteristics among the citizens of any society. Some are cleverer or more cultured. Some are more suited to the pursuit of the moral and the intellectual life, while

others have greater aptitudes for attaining wealth or power. No one with eyes in his head can or will deny the existence of these human differences. But what is often argued is that the basic similarities among human beings outweigh and are more significant than the differences that separate them. "As to the strength of body, the weakest has strength enough to kill the strongest, either by secret machination, or by confederacy with others . . . " Thomas Hobbes said, "and as to faculties of the mind, . . . I find yet a greater equality amongst men, than that of strength." And in addition to physical and mental similarities, it has been pointed out that men share the same basic needs. All people need to give and receive love and affection; all people need the respect of others and the feeling that they are performing a useful function in society. To be sure, it may be argued that some people will be satisfied with humbler occupations or will welcome the chance to conform to authority. Yet such a view must not be carried too far. No person wants to be the slave of another; indeed, no man wants to be deprived of a vote or a voice in his government if he sees that others have such privileges. All in all, the question of whether men are on the whole similar or different is a question of interpreting the observable facts. There may be no agreement on what the facts mean or even which are the most important facts. Nevertheless, the debate can only be carried on by constant recourse to the past and present experience of man in society.

EQUALITY AND INEQUALITY "The metaphysical and alchemical legislators," Edmund Burke argued, " . . . have attempted to confound all sorts of citizens, as well as they could, into one homogeneous mass." Attempts at artificial equalization ignore the fact that some men are "naturally" superior to others, and these fortunate individuals ought to have a preferred status in society and greater power in the conduct of government. The question of who is superior and who is inferior is resolved not by looking at the facts but by having recourse to philosophy. Such a philosophy may state that some people are the "elect" of God and therefore superior to those of their fellow men who were not so chosen. Another philosophy may postulate that the social organism, like the human organism, will have both physical and moral qualities; thus it follows that the population will have natural gradations, with some citizens doing the manual labor and others carrying out the higher callings. And if society is an organism, it follows that all its members cannot be equal by birth or talent. Arguments over whether all men are or are not equal are difficult to settle. For the disputants have almost invariably made up their minds beforehand as a result of being committed to a particular philosophy. The person who believes all men are equal will usually stress the observable similarities among individuals. The person who believes they are unequal will stress the differences. However, it is important to note that the citing of facts does not prove or disprove a philosophical view. Facts can illustrate such a viewpoint and can convey its meaning in a vivid way. But there will never be enough facts to validate or verify either the philosophy of equality or the philosophy of inequality. Temperament, emotion, and personal interest cause men to espouse one view or the other.

EQUAL PEOPLE AND UNEQUAL PEOPLE Another problem arises in discussions of equality. This involves the question of which people we have in mind when we say that some individuals are or are not the "equals" of others. This has practical implications, for it entails a consideration of the power relationships between groups in a society. Two quite different situations can prevail:

I	II
"Unequals" = a powerful minority	"Equals" = the powerful majority
"Equals" = the powerless majority	"Unequals" = a powerless minority

In situation I, when it emerges that some people are "unequal" to others, it means that there exists a privileged or powerful group of citizens that possesses qualities or positions superior to those enjoyed by everyone else. In this instance, the people in the majority are apt to argue against those inequalities, demanding that the minority's privileges be abolished and that power be redistributed in a more equitable manner. However in situation II, when it is said that some people are "unequal" to others, it means that society contains one or more minority groups who suffer oppression or discrimination at the hands of their fellow citizens. Here it is those in the minority who demand an end to inequality. But in both situations, the classes lacking privileges or power say to the people in more favored positions, "We are as good as you are!" And often that outcry carries overtones of envy and enmity. At the same time, there are frequently some individuals belonging to either the minority in situation I or the majority in situation II who have uneasy consciences about their privileged positions. These people gaze down on those less fortunate than themselves and say, "You are as good as we are!" (Or even, "There but for the Grace of God go I!") In short, the efforts to do away with inequality can come from quite different sources and be spurred by quite varying motives.

EQUALITY OF OPPORTUNITY? Many people who find themselves uneasy over the prospect of an equalitarian society still profess their support for equality of opportunity. Such an idea, if put into practice, would mean that everyone would start out with pretty much the same chance for achieving success in life. One or two observations may be made concerning the assumptions underlying this proposal. First of all, not all people begin with equal opportunities now. The main reason is that some children come from backgrounds providing an inadequate preparation for the contests ahead. If a "starting line" is visualized, a large number of youngsters begin behind that mark, while others actually start a few paces ahead (diagram *a*). If "equality of opportunity" is to be achieved, then not only will some individuals have to be brought up to the starting line before the race begins, but others will have to be sent back to that point so the competition will be a fair one (diagram *b*). But not many parents who are in a position to give their children extra privileges will consent to sending their offspring back to a common starting point. Yet until that happens, it is difficult to see how opportunity can be made equal.

The outcome of equal opportunity

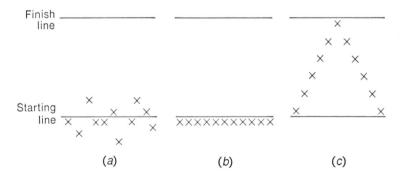

Second, let us assume that somehow everyone does begin at the same line (diagram *b*). The whistle blows, and people commence to do the best that their talents and temperaments permit. By the time the race is halfway over, it will emerge that some people have done better than others (diagram *c*). Those with more intelligence or perseverance (or whatever aptitudes or achievements are needed for success) will end up with higher positions or greater rewards. Thus equality of opportunity in fact produces an inequalitarian result. It may be a "fairer" outcome, but it still has some individuals remaining at the bottom. The difference is that now it can be said that those left behind "deserve" to be where they are. Therefore it should be made clear that the argument for equal opportunity places a premium on competition, and it conceives of a system in which some people win success while others are considered failures. For this reason, "equality of opportunity" should not be construed as a plea for equality. While it advocates the same start for everyone, it assumes that members of the society will end up arrayed in some kind of hierarchical order.

THE RIGHTS OF MAN "The sum of all we drive at," John Locke wrote, "is that every man enjoys the same rights that are granted to others." A "right" is freedom: it is the liberty of an individual to engage in one or another kind of behavior. The right of free speech means that a person can say what he pleases without being silenced by someone else. The right of private property means that a person may own his own business and conduct it in a manner that he thinks suitable to its growth and profitability. Rights, however, are a special kind of freedom because they must be accorded to all men equally. If some people are allowed to own property and others are not, then property ownership is a *privilege* and not a right. The chief characteristic of a right, then, is its equalitarian basis. But even here theory and practice may be rather far apart. For example, the right of free speech means that all citizens can say their piece without interference by the government or other citizens. For the average person this means he can climb on the proverbial soapbox and exhort all those within earshot. However, some citizens own newspapers or magazines and it is clear that their opinions will reach many more people. The right of free speech implies that *any* citizen can go into the business of publishing a newspaper or a magazine. Yet it hardly needs to be said that the average person simply does not have the money to set up a *New York Times* or a Columbia Broadcasting System. Despite the equalitarian character of the right, there will still be some voices that will be heard more loudly and more frequently than others. By the same token, every citizen is "free" to start up his own General Motors Corporation.

THE SOURCES OF RIGHTS   Where do rights come from? There are, generally speaking, two schools of thought on this question. The first was incomparably expressed in a passage familiar to everyone, "We hold these truths to be self-evident,—that all men are created equal; that they are endowed by their Creator with certain unalienable rights. . . . " This is the theory of "natural rights" and it postulates that all men are *born* with certain rights and that these rights are the gift of God or some other supernatural power. What is being suggested here is that in order to lead a full life and in order to fulfill their potentialities as human beings, citizens must be guaranteed certain freedoms. Moreover, a person possesses these "natural rights" at all times and in all places. They belong to him because he is a human individual, and they still remain his even if a government or society denies him the freedoms he thinks he ought to have.

The big stumbling block for natural rights has been to find some way of determining just what they are and how they should be applied in varying circumstances. One may postulate that natural rights do indeed exist and that they are vested by God in every individual. But suppose that a citizen claims that he has a natural right to walk the streets with no clothes on? We can ask him who told him that this form of behavior is actually a natural right. He may reply that he has pondered the matter, in a manner befitting a rational being, and has concluded that God gave man sun and air so he might enjoy those natural blessings. He may even quote a passage or two from Scripture thus lending authority to his argument. It is very difficult to refute such a claim. There is no way of testing whether a claimed right is "natural," or whether it is simply a personal interest that an individual wishes to gratify. Nor can it be said that a right becomes "natural" in character if a majority of the people think this is the case. For the Voice of God does not necessarily emanate from the mouths of the multitude. Moreover, society does not have a tribunal of judges in direct communication with the Deity, who can decide which claimed rights are "natural" and which are not.

Hence, there has emerged the view that rights are to be found on the statute books and only there. Hobbes wrote, "The liberty of a subject lieth only in those things, which in regulating their actions, the sovereign hath pretermitted [i.e. not expressly forbade]." This means that rights are made by men and that they have their origins in the legislative, judicial, and constitutional processes of a society. A citizen may be said to have the right to free speech only if a law or a constitution grants him this right, or if he can show that there is no law or constitutional provision expressly forbidding the making of speeches. In this way, new rights may be created and old rights can be amended or even abolished. Indeed, rights are gained in the same way that laws are enacted or constitutions revised. Furthermore, courts play a significant role in interpreting laws and constitutions, by telling citizens what rights they do and do not have. This theory of rights makes the definition of individual freedom very much part of the political process. For groups, acting through courts and legislatures, will plainly try to have their interests or aspirations guaranteed to them by having them transformed into rights. Such a view may be less uplifting than the natural rights theory, but it is at least a more accurate description of how people behave.

THE ENFORCEMENT OF RIGHTS One of the continuing problems of politics is that although rights may exist in theory they are not guaranteed in practice. There can be several reasons for this. One is that the agencies of law enforcement are often more concerned with maintaining social order than they are with protecting particular rights of individuals. Or, on the other hand, such agencies may be so inefficient or understaffed or lacking in power that they are unable to guarantee the rights of citizens. On other occasions enforcement officials may be less than sympathetic to the people whose rights they are supposed to protect. What this adds up to is that rights are not self-enforcing. Finally, it is not simply government that grants or withholds rights in actual practice. Society, by exerting overt pressures and sanctions, can cause individuals to refrain from exercising rights that they theoretically possess. These observations on the enforcement of rights can be applied both to "natural rights" and to rights that have a basis in law.

SOVEREIGNTY AND POWER

The discussion of rights demonstrated that legal authority is not always enforced and that power must underpin the words inscribed on statute books. Nevertheless, it is important to emphasize the role of law in politics and society. Most laws are obeyed by most citizens most of the time, and nearly everyone grants that the rule of law is vital for civilized life.

SOVEREIGNTY   "The legislator in all commonwealths is the only sovereign," Thomas Hobbes continued. "For the legislator is he that makes the law." This may appear to be a truism, but it has not always been the case in the past and there is no assurance that it will always be so in the future. A society can have but a single "sovereign," that is, only one institution or set of institutions can be the ultimate source of law. If there are two legislatures, one in the East and one in the West, each attempting to make laws for the entire country, then it is obvious that chaos will be the only result. Virtually all societies that have tried to become nation-states in the modern world have undergone the tràvails of creating a single and unified sovereign. Problems of this sort continue to plague underdeveloped countries, especially if they are seeking to create a nation out of what was previously a conglomeration of tribes and villages. For sovereignty to become established there must emerge a respect for law on the part of citizens, and this means their acknowledging that one particular authority is the source of all laws. Individuals must give up—voluntarily or under compulsion—sectional loyalties, and they must take a new and expanded view of citizenship. The theory of sovereignty is a first principle of government because until a sovereign is established there can be no meaningful talk of freedom or equality or rights. For these values are created by law and exist only as long as law is an object of respect.

Is it possible to identify the sovereign in any state or society? That is, can one locate the "seat" of sovereignty in a definitive way? For many years such a treasure hunt was a pastime of students of politics, but interest in it has waned and probably for good reason. It may be asked where sovereignty lies, for example, in the United States. The national government is not the sovereign lawmaker, for certain powers are reserved to the states and these may not be taken away. Within the national government, the President and the two chambers of the legislature must all participate in enacting laws. It cannot be said that any one of the three branches is "supreme." Moreover, the Supreme Court may overrule statutes and nullify executive orders. But it does not have the last word because the composition of and the rules governing the court's jurisdiction are subject to legislative revision. All these relationships can be altered if the states amend the Constitution. But this power has been exercised fewer than 30 times in almost two hundred years, and not usually on issues of the most crucial character. One might conclude, therefore, that the people of the United States are the sovereign because they elect or control the makers of public policy. However, this begs the question of which people we are talking about and at which times. For the people participate in the lawmaking process only in specified ways and at certain junctures. Perhaps the Constitution itself is the sovereign; however, a little reflection shows that it is a piece of parchment always standing in need of interpretation.

The real answer is that sovereignty is not something that can be identified or discovered. It is, on the contrary, a *process.* In other words, it is the interaction of specified individuals and institutions according to specified rules of procedure. Laws are enacted, cases are decided, and constitutions are amended only if certain paths of action are followed by people in a certain specified position. The process of sovereignty, therefore, is more concerned with *how* laws are passed than with *what* they say. This is why many theorists believe that a constitution must be the foundation of any government. For such a document lays down the basic rules by which laws are made and attempts to ensure that the whims and caprices of politicians are checked by orderly procedures.

WHO HAS THE POWER? "In all republics, however organized," Machiavelli wrote, "there are never more than forty or fifty citizens who attain a position that entitles them to command." This view suggests that while lawyers may muse over questions of legality and sovereignty, the key issue is who has the real power in politics. Even in the best of democracies, where the people believe that they govern themselves, it can still be suggested that power gravitates (or ascends) to a small elite. Indeed, even in a representative system in which lawmakers are popularly elected, it can be shown that a ruling circle usually emerges. Constitutions, therefore, are less important than the men who are able to shape them in ways of their own choosing. Legislatures may enact laws according to specified procedures, but the real issue is which individuals and groups secure laws that promote their own interests.

This elite theory is based on several premises, all worth considering. The first is that the mass of the people is usually apathetic about politics. They do not want to govern themselves and would not know how to do so even if they wanted to. In this view, all that the people need to be given is material security, a sense of self-respect, and some outlets for emotional expression. If the economic well-being of a population can be achieved, then its ego can be boosted by flattery and the manipulation of patriotic and similar symbols. Indeed, many analysts feel that most citizens *want* to be followers and that they are relieved when authoritative leaders appear on the scene. Coincidental with these observations is the perception that as political life becomes more organized certain tendencies come into play. Thus popular movements turn into established parties, and these in turn become rigid bureaucracies. The same evolution occurs in government itself and with other social institutions. The making of decisions develops into a specialized process, and only those with expert information can participate in a serious way. Thus leaders become a select group, separated from the average citizens and possessed of disproportionate power. Who are these leaders? As was pointed out in an earlier chapter, they may have one of several aptitudes. One such leader will have a talent for projecting his personality and amassing a following around him as an individual. Another may be an able administrator, with the ability to execute far-reaching policies by manipulating a complex organization. But the point is that no matter what the country or the period in history, this theory asserts that effective power will always be in a few hands. This means that democracy, defined as popular self-government, is a myth. However, it does not mean that all governments are tyrannies. For an oligarchic system need not oppress the mass of citizens, and the best of them will make an explicit point not to do so.

Governments must exercise power and most will agree that such power should be wielded by rational men. The real argument comes over the question whether men of reason form only a small minority or if there is a sufficiency of reason in the entire society to warrant an attempt at self-government. This issue lies at the heart of the controversy over democracy, and that theory will be turned to next.

REVIEW QUESTIONS

1. Is government the only institution that can deprive an individual of his freedom?

2. How can someone be "forced to be free"?

3. Can a person think he is free and yet not be?

4. How can men be considered equal despite obvious differences in attributes and achievements?

5. What is the difference between a right and a privilege?

6. Is there one person, or group of persons, in a society who may be said to be sovereign?

4 IDEOLOGIES AND INTERESTS

Properly understood, political theory bears a close connection to the important issues of political life. It is often tempting for students of politics to preoccupy themselves with the trivial, if only because more minute subjects are easier to handle. By the same token, there is a tendency to delve into conditions and conflicts of the political past, for those controversies have already been settled and may be described without undue difficulty. In addition, there are commentators who concentrate on questions of current or topical concern, selecting these problems because they happen to arouse popular and often undiscriminating interest. These pitfalls must be avoided, for if political theory is to serve a serious purpose it must discuss enduring issues. That is, it must focus on questions that recur in political life and that transcend the particular experiences of specific societies and epochs.

This is more easily said than done. For the significant problems of politics cannot always be analyzed or evaluated in a dispassionate way. A theorist should serve only a single master: the truth. His self-chosen mission is to describe and explain the conduct of politics and to outline how politics ought to be pursued if the general welfare is to be promoted.

But the more important a political issue becomes, the more likely it will be that ideology will intrude itself into theory. This is inevitable. What must be said, in consequence, is that anyone who reads the literature of politics must be on constant guard. He must be able to detect ideological intrusions and to ask how and why they managed to creep in. This warning is especially important in the case of the theories that are to follow. For it is all but impossible to discuss democracy, welfare, and revolution in a dispassionate tone. Emotions and interests, along with distortions and rationalizations, are constantly at play in this arena. Nor is this to be deplored or condemned out of hand. The intervention of these altogether human qualities gives life to the debate and reminds us once again that serious men think these questions important.

THE DEBATE OVER DEMOCRACY

MOB RULE "When the poor win, the result is democracy," Plato wrote. "They will kill some of the opposite party, banish others, and grant the rest an equal share in civil rights and government." This theory, a popular one throughout history, defines democracy as mob rule. Every society has more poor people than rich people, more who are uneducated than who are educated. If political power is distributed equally throughout the population, then sheer quantity of numbers will win out over quality. The populace, led by people much like themselves, will overwhelm the cultured, well-to-do, or well-born minorities that previously held high status in the community. The masses, furthermore, are unable or unwilling to appreciate the values such minorities have protected or the functions they performed on behalf of all of society. Hence what results is not simply majority rule, but in fact "the tyranny of the majority."

Democracy in this process does not have to be accompanied by violence. The redistribution of power can be gradual, with each decade giving more of a say to the average citizen and his neighbors. In the same way, the expropriation of property, the dilution of privilege, and the downgrading of culture may take place by stages rather than at one seizure. The gradual growth of equalitarian democracy is a subtle development; and after a progression of concessions, it is virtually impossible to withdraw those rights that have been handed over to the majority.

DOES THE MOB RULE? At the same time, it is argued that popular democracy usually has a short life and it seldom allows majority rule for an extended period. "The people always put forward a single champion of their interests, whom they nurse to greatness," Plato continued. "Here, plainly enough, is the root from which despotism invariably springs." A mob, in actual fact, is poorly equipped for conducting the business of government. Whether its members are roaming the streets, gathered in the marketplace, or sitting in their homes they cannot make policy or carry out programs. The experience has been that a single man or a small group of men are elevated to positions of leadership, and from this eminence they presumably exercise power in the name of the people. Should such a leader be called a despot? He may look that way to those citizens who have suffered from the advent of democracy. But to the populace he may be a hero, a savior, or even a saint, whose likeness looks down from every wall. However, as he or his successors consolidate the fruits of popular rule, he may act ruthlessly toward individuals who were among his original supporters but who develop misgivings about his methods. Yet so long as leaders maintain the support of the masses, they usually have a free hand in selecting their lieutenants and in administering the governmental apparatus.

The conclusion must be that despotism is not incompatible with at least one conception of democracy. Leaders "represent" their follow-ings after a fashion and the masses feel that their interests are being attended to. Such a democracy has little room for individual dissenters or opposition parties. Nor can it contain deliberative legislatures or an independent judiciary. What must be said is that if it has a popular base, the people who make up this constituency have a fairly uncomplicated view of politics and a rather rudimentary conception of human freedom. But as this description can be applied to most people in the world it ought not to be surprising that popular democracy, coupled with authoritarian leadership, is a common form of government.

THE RATIONAL MAJORITY "There is this to be said for the Many," Aristotle replied. "Each of them by himself may not be of a good quality; but when they all come together it is possible that they may surpass— collectively and as a body, although not individually—the quality of the best few." In Plato's conception, the majority was considered incompetent to govern, being unable to appreciate the finer things of life or to take a long-range view on questions of public policy. Aristotle's approach suggests that the Many, when considered as a collectivity, possesses a wisdom of its own that may be superior to that of any minority. For one thing, it has been pointed out that there may be several minority groups in the community, each of which feels itself to be of superior quality. Quite frequently, for example, the well-to-do will disagree with the intellectuals on what constitutes a rational course of action. By allowing the majority to govern, the dilemma of deciding which minority is "really" superior can be avoided.

How can one find wisdom in the majority? For this group often has inadequate education, frequently inclines to excess, and has been known to select as its leaders the most irresponsible of demagogues. The answer is to be found, first of all, by returning to a theory of human nature. While the majority has occasionally acted oppressively when it secures power, this usually stems from the fact that it was itself long a victim of exploitation. Once their own memories of oppression have faded away, this theory continues, the goodness and rationality inherent in the common man will have a chance to develop. Furthermore, these underlying qualities evidence themselves best when men and women deliberate collectively. For in the course of discussion they exchange facts and ideas and come to appreciate the interests and opinions of others. In this way, the majority emerges with a sense of what its own needs are and, hopefully, what is best for society as a whole.

ARISTOCRATIC LEADERS AND DEMOCRATIC FOLLOWERS "No government," John Stuart Mill wrote, ". . . ever did or could rise above mediocrity except insofar as the sovereign Many have let themselves be guided (which in the best of times they have always done) by the counsels and influence of a more highly gifted and instructed One or Few." Here it is recalled that the majority frequently shows itself willing to pick as leaders the best minds and talents in society, even though those individuals come from a different class or ethnic group than themselves. In these cases, the common man displays a commendable deference to his betters; he acknowledges his own limitations and willingly permits men of superior abilities to assume positions of power. Thus if a theorist speaks of the "good sense" of the majority, part of what he may have in mind is that ordinary citizens have the wisdom to know quality when they see it and to elevate it to places of leadership.

This conception of democracy may be called "representative democracy" in contradistinction to the "popular democracy" discussed earlier. In a representative democracy the people have the right to vote, but on the whole they allow the men and women they place in office to make policy and run the government. That is, citizens remain content to elect their rulers and pass judgment on them at periodic elections. But between those elections the majority permits its representatives to do what they think is best. The majority, in this system, forbears from having intense opinions on every political issue and refrains from exerting too continuous a measure of pressure on its elected officeholders. While a degree of such communication may be permissible, to remind representatives of their constituents' sentiments, it must not get out of hand. The reason for this is that lawmakers and administrators must be able to give reasoned reflection to policies and programs, and they cannot be stampeded by the clamor of the moment. Indeed, if superior men are selected for office they should be allowed to exercise their knowledge and intelligence in an atmosphere of objectivity and calm.

MAJORITY RULE VERSUS MINORITY RIGHTS   "For a people that governs and is well regulated by laws will be stable, prudent and grateful, as much so, and even more, according to my opinion, than a prince," Machiavelli concluded. While it is well to have faith in the stability and prudence of the majority, it is also important to ensure that majority power will be restrained by certain basic laws. The view that a representative democracy is a "republican" form of government also implies that the entire political system will be overarched by a constitution designed to protect individual liberty and minority rights. The power of the majority, therefore, is not unlimited. There are certain things that neither the majority nor its elected representatives are allowed to do. Nevertheless, such constitutional guarantees only will survive if the members of the majority are reasonably tolerant of dissenters and properly deferential to the institutions that seek to uphold the rights of individuals. When such tolerance and deference are not forthcoming, the whole theory of limited majority rule is in jeopardy.

Which rights of individuals and minorities can legitimately claim constitutional protection? This question covers one of the great debates of democratic theory. The well-to-do may assert that they have a right to keep all the money they have earned or inherited. Political dissenters may insist that they have a right to demonstrate for radical changes in the economic and governmental system. Intellectuals may contend that the amenities of high culture deserve greater support and encouragement. And members of groups that have suffered from discrimination may call for special attention or even preferential treatment. Most of these minority assertions tend to conflict with majority sentiment, and it is not easy to ascertain which of the claims deserve recognition. One of the reasons why courts of justice are supposed to remain independent of political pressure is so they can decide who has what rights, without having to worry about the majority opinion of the moment.

PROMOTING THE GENERAL WELFARE

No one is "against" welfare. It is not easy to find a reputable theorist who believes that poverty is to be praised or misery eulogized. The real question concerns the means by which a society may best promote the general welfare. If the plight of the poor and underprivileged is looked upon as a "problem," the arguments revolve over which of various solutions best coincide with values such as justice or progress. And while the substantive issue may be economic in character, it is clear that political policies play a key role. For the economy and the system of government stand in integral relation to one another, and the contours of the one will inevitably be shaped by the outlines of the other.

PROPERTY, PERSONALITY, AND PROGRESS   "The great and chief end of men's uniting into commonwealths, and putting themselves under government, is the preservation of their property," John Locke wrote. According to this view, the freedom to own property is a natural right belonging to all citizens and it is the obligation of government to guarantee that right. This theory of property is very much bound up with the idea that each individual ought to develop his own personality. If a citizen is to express himself as a free person he must have some measure of economic security. The property owner can, by building up possessions that are uniquely his own, create not only a source of livelihood but also a defensive bulwark against the rest of society. That is, the person of property has in effect a "fenced-off" area where he can do as he pleases. Moreover, it is through his private property than an individual can express his personality. He may build a business or farm his land in ways of his own devising, thus imposing his character on an enterprise in a unique manner. Related to this is the fact that through property a person can secure a sense of "identity." In an organic society this identity comes to an individual through his family inheritance and by his fulfilling a settled role in the community. In an atomistic society, however, identity is more difficult to establish because attachments are transitory and roles in a constant state of flux. Thus through the ownership of property an individual can shape an identity for himself by merging his personality with his land or business, creating a focus by which others know him and by which, indeed, he comes to know himself. Owning property, then, is not simply an economic right. It also brings in its train psychological benefits of profound importance.

For this reason, it has been argued, government must protect the right of citizens to acquire and own property. The state should remain aloof from the economic realm, permitting individuals to buy, sell, and build their fortunes. Only in a marketplace unhampered by government regulation can each person exercise his talents and express his personality. Furthermore, by refraining from intervening, the government is actually promoting economic progress. Through free competition, prices are kept low and the quality of service grows better. Because innovation is a matter of individual decisions, new products develop and more jobs are created. Entrepreneurs take risks, with penalties for the losers as well as rewards for the winners. However, the overall result is a rising standard of living for everyone and an increase in the wealth of nations. Thus, while the poor may have less than the rich, the material level of the poor is constantly rising to new heights. In addition, new individuals can begin new enterprises, using their talents to better their condition. Such an economy provides incentives for progress and, by its workings, serves the welfare of all.

AN ECONOMIC ROLE FOR GOVERNMENT "The business of government is to promote the happiness of society," Jeremy Bentham wrote. And this includes "the power which takes for its object the introduction of positive good." Why is it suggested that the government must take a "positive" role in the economy? The reply to this question is that the workings of the unregulated market may in fact not provide a rising standard of living for everyone. Not everyone has sufficient talent or good fortune to become a successful entrepreneur; and those whose rewards are comparatively meager tend to be less than satisfied with the workings of the competitive system. Nor will it do to point out that the society is progressing or that the average person's standard of living has been rising. For most people set their expectations by observing the condition of life enjoyed by those better off than themselves, and they are not mollified by statistical tables telling them that they "never had it so good." Furthermore, it is frequently argued that the free market does not always provide jobs for everyone who wants to work, indeed it does not always provide essential services. The sum of this analysis is that government must play a positive role in the economy.

These economic functions can be quite varied. They may involve redistributing society's wealth, by taxing the well-to-do and then giving free or low-cost services to the poor. Or government officials may tell businessmen what they can or cannot do, with the intention of creating a more rational system of production and distribution. In these instances, the assumption is that an "invisible hand" does *not* automatically produce prosperity, so the visible hand of government must act as a referee and often as a rule maker. On occasion, too, agencies of government will enter the marketplace, manufacturing goods or supplying services—such as housing or electric power—that private enterprises have been unwilling to provide. In all these instances, the theory is that government can be an agency of public service. While some businessmen may be harmed by redistributive or regulatory measures, this is counterbalanced by the many citizens who gain greater security in the process. This view suggests that only if individuals have such security can they begin to experience the good life themselves and give a decent start to their children.

PROPERTY AND THE PROPERTYLESS   The right to property, while theoretically open to everyone on equal terms, tends to have meaning for only a portion of the population. The role that government will play in the economic realm depends, in the final analysis, on the attitudes of those citizens who are *not* property owners. (And by "property," it should be added, theorists mean more than a car, a house, or a modest portfolio of stocks. Property really connotes the ownership of a business, a farm, or shares having sufficient earnings to provide a quite comfortable income.) If they are relatively content with the rewards offered them by the economic system, they will not insist on a substantial measure of governmental intervention. However, if they are not satisfied, they may demand that government become a much more active force in the economy. Whether the rights of property ownership will be safeguarded depends, then, on how many citizens feel that their welfare is being promoted by the workings of the free enterprise system. If a majority feel that they are suffering injustice, then the chances are good that more government intervention will be forthcoming. One of the consequences of democracy is that people seek to solve their economic problems by political means.

OBEDIENCE, OPPRESSION, AND REVOLUTION

OBEDIENCE TO AUTHORITY   "It would indeed be dangerous, both for the community and for its rulers, if individuals were, upon private initiative, to attempt the death of those who govern, albeit tyrannically," St. Thomas Aquinas warned. "The consequence of such presumption is more likely to be the loss of a good king to the community than any benefit from the suppression of tyranny." The argument against disobedience—whether it involves ignoring a traffic signal or embarking upon violent revolution—is a powerful one. One of the most important characteristics of government, whether benevolent or tyrannical, is that it is a means of preserving order. All men want society to be an orderly place. They want to live under a system of rules and want life to be reasonably predictable. Citizens like to know that the mail will be delivered on time, that police will protect them from criminals, that tomorrow their currency will buy pretty much what it bought today. Any individual, or group of individuals, who undertakes to disobey the law endangers the entire edifice of civilized life, the theory postulates. The obligation to obey authority is often annoying and occasionally requires countenancing what appear to be instances of injustice. At the same time, disobedience can bring consequences harmful not only to society, but also to the very individuals who thought that acts of resistance would bring a new era of freedom and justice.

Moreover, if disobedience is condoned, then bad men may break good laws no less than may good men break bad ones. If revolution is sanctioned, then good rulers may be toppled no less than tyrants. If citizens are granted a "right of revolution," it should not be surprising that all who foment rebellion will claim to act under this mantle. In addition, the aftermath of revolution is frequently marked by the advent of a new autocracy that proceeds to deprive whole groups and classes of their liberty. Old tyrants are replaced by new oppressors, and the freedoms won by some are paid for by the injustices visited on others.

Nevertheless, only a few societies in history or even in the world today have been so organized that political change can take place without violence. Not much more than a fraction of nations have regular elections at which citizens may replace their rulers in an orderly manner. By the same token, it is only in these few countries that the man in the street can work to have bad laws repealed and ones more to his liking enacted. Put another way, in most parts of the world constitutional channels for change do not exist. This means that the likelihood of disobedience on the part of disaffected citizens will continue extensive in scope and persuasive in thrust.

WHY MEN REVOLT "At a certain stage of their development, the material productive forces of society come into conflict with the existing relations of production . . . " Karl Marx wrote. "Then begins an epoch of social revolution." This, the most famous of all revolutionary theories, explains social and political upheaval by analyzing the economic and technological elements in human relationships. According to Marxist theory, there are periods in history when the stage of technological development ("the material productive forces") are in harmony with the way in which the economy ("the existing relations of production") is organized. Thus the feudal economic system was well-suited to a primitive agricultural technology. Or a capitalist economic system harmonized well with small-scale manufacturing and a technology based on steam power. At such intervals in history the workers see no injustice in an economy where only a few own property, because that particular economic organization apparently goes best with the technological instruments at hand. Trouble arises, this theory goes on to say, when the workers begin to perceive an inherent conflict between the "forces" of production and the "relations" of production. What happens, is that as technology advances, the workers become more sophisticated and begin to sense an irrationality in the system. If they work in a capitalist economy, for example, they may begin to ask why they labor for a pittance whereas others who do not work reap the profits. Indeed, they may begin to conclude that whereas a mass-production factory is a rational agency of production, the way in which the economy is organized lacks a parallel logic. In order to bring matters into harmony, the workers organize a revolutionary movement, the purpose of which is to displace those in power and replace them with a system compatible with the prevailing technology. Marxist theory, therefore, is more than an "economic determinism"; if anything, it focuses chiefly on the course of technological development. And it is not simply a capitalist economic system that makes men revolutionaries; for machines, factories, and the processes of production also help to shape their minds and foster their discontents.

This theory is an attempt to explain why citizens become dissatisfied with established social and political arrangements. It is both a theory of history and a psychological conception, and no one can deny that it has been singularly influential over the past century. The Marxist analysis assumes that a property-owning minority (the bourgeoisie) exploits the propertyless majority. However it may take a long time before this majority even realizes it is being exploited; indeed they will only come to this realization once they develop a "class consciousness." What makes them conscious of their true class position is the impact of their work on their lives; in particular, the constant exposure to the forces of technology, which define their role in the total system.

Most commentators acknowledge that the Marxist explanation needs some updating. For one thing, the important revolutions of our time have taken place in nonindustrial societies. In these instances, the workers were not exposed to mass-production technology, and thus had no chance to juxtapose the "rationality" of the machines with the "irrationality" of capitalist ownership. If feelings of exploitation have emerged in the minds of peasants and residents of rural villages, they arise from other bases. Not the least of these is nationalism, the growing desire on the part of emerging societies to throw off foreign overlords and to chart their own destinies.

THE CASE FOR CONFRONTATION Placing a premium on stability presupposes that the major outlines of the political and economic system should be preserved. Thus even the argument for reform assumes that these changes will be confined to rearranging prevailing processes. But not all citizens find themselves able to accept the structure they see rising about them. In their perception, an emphasis on stability means preserving a system which is essentially inequitable. Moreover, political institutions seem so tied to an established order that elections and legislation have little effect on the major injustices of the society. What are described as reforms either strengthen already dominant groups, or they apply adhesive tape where thoroughgoing surgery is needed. The quest for stability, in this view, masks the fact that a society can have selfishness, cruelty, and even violence institutionalized in its routine functioning.

Given these premises, it may be said that stability perpetuates classes and modes of conduct that induce irrationality and corrupt human character. If change must remain confined to such measures as can be effected through the ballot box, individuals will never have the opportunity to develop their potentialities for an expressive and creative life. Instead, they will continue as the kinds of persons the prevailing system wishes them to be. According to this analysis, the conventional politics of parties and interest groups never exercise real influence over the decisions that give society its dominant shape. For the basic structure is only marginally affected by the ration of power allotted to those holding public office. Thus if the system is to be altered, other means must be employed. Just how far countries accustomed to stressing stability can accommodate or contain resistance of this sort remains to be seen. But it seems clear that more citizens than in the recent past now find themselves rejecting ideas and institutions that were once taken for granted.

REVIEW QUESTIONS

1. If democracy is viewed as the tyranny of the majority, who are the tyrants and who are the tyrannized?

2. What is the difference between popular democracy and representative democracy?

3. Why is the right of private property thought to be important?

4. When does the government intervene in the economy?

5. Have citizens any obligation to obey their government?

6. What causes revolutions?

5 HUMAN NATURE AND POLITICAL AUTHORITY

Not a few commentators have lamented the fact that there are no American political theorists comparable to those produced by the European tradition. Great Britain can claim Locke, Burke, Bentham, Hobbes, and Mill. France has given us Rousseau and Tocqueville. Germany may point to Hegel and Marx. And Italy has Machiavelli.

Somehow or for some reason, the philosophical impulse has failed to flower in American soil. There are explanations for this state of affairs. It has been pointed out that we are still a comparatively young nation and that in the fullness of time there will develop creative minds and audiences receptive to mature ideas. It has also been suggested that Americans have been preoccupied with building a continent, with the practical aspects of life necessarily emphasized. Nor can it be denied that during the past century both America and the world have been in an unsettled condition; a theory written today may well be obsolete by tomorrow.

PHILOSOPHY AND PUBLICITY

Nevertheless, Americans have no reason to be apologetic. The Federalist, written at the birth of the Republic in 1787 and 1788, may be regarded as a major contribution to political theory. There is, to be sure, some understandable hesitation about placing it on a shelf alongside the august books of the European tradition. For one thing, The Federalist originated not as a book but as a series of newspaper articles. And these articles had not a single author but rather three contributors, each of whom put forward his own ideas in his essays in the series. Thus, The Federalist may be criticized for being aimed at a large and popular audience, for being put together hurriedly to meet newspaper deadlines, for embracing varied and even opposing viewpoints due to multiple authorship. Yet the overriding fact is that in spite of these handicaps the articles contain ideas of major and lasting significance for politics. Indeed, the pressures operating on the authors worked to bring out the best in them, and that in itself is a lesson of no small importance.

The Constitutional Convention met in the summer of 1787, and it succeeded in drawing up a document that would transform thirteen loosely confederated states into a single federal republic. Upon the adjournment of that gathering, the delegates dispersed and turned their attention to the practical business of getting the document ratified. One of the key states, then as now, was New York. To convince the voters of New York that they should support the proposed constitution, a major campaign of popular persuasion was necessary. In consequence, John Jay, Alexander Hamilton, and James Madison set pen to paper and wrote 85 articles for publication in various New York newspapers. These frankly propagandistic columns had as their purpose winning votes for the new constitution. All the articles were brief and all were anonymous. Each one was signed "Publius," but we are now able to assign authorship to the individual papers. We know that Hamilton was responsible for 51 of them, that Madison wrote 26, Jay wrote 5, and 3 were collaborative efforts by the two principal authors.

Reading these articles raises some fascinating questions about the art of political persuasion. As has been noted, these were newspaper columns and were clearly addressed to a large and quite ordinary readership. After all, ratification of the Constitution in New York State would be in the hands of an electorate extending deep into the population. Although not all adult males were allowed to vote—and no women were—the franchise still embraced many citizens of modest backgrounds and limited education. Nevertheless, the articles contain all manner of historical and academic allusions. There are references to writers like Plato, Montesquieu, Grotius, and Hume; there are discussions of ancient Greece, Renaissance Italy, and Reformation England. The modern reader may well wonder about the worldliness of the average newspaper buyer in those years; and he cannot help but compare the elevated level of the *Federalist* arguments with the mode of discussion that prevails today. There are, as will be seen, extended analyses of major questions of political theory, embracing human nature, social structure, and governmental authority. How much of this could be understood by the typical citizen of that time? We really do not know. But what can be said is that the *Federalist* authors also devoted ample space to the practical considerations that clearly concerned the voters. If they waxed philosophical, they also went far to allay the fears that a unitary national government would destroy the powers of the states. If they drew their analogies from history, they also proceeded to demonstrate that the new constitution would bring order and prosperity to an emerging nation.

In contrast to the ideas of the European tradition, *The Federalist* has a direct link with specific political institutions and social conditions. That is, the authors were content to deal with problems that were uniquely American. They did not prescribe conduct or institutions for all men everywhere. The Constitution was an American instrument, with institutions intended to solve American problems in an American context. The upshot is that the theories in *The Federalist* were never far removed from practical matters of government and politics. A generalization about human nature, for example, was to be used to justify a bicameral legislature. A reflection on political authority was to be offered as a reason for a unitary executive. *The Federalist,* therefore, served as a bridge between theory and practice. And it was because its authors were men who combined scholarly learning and practical experience that such a transition could be effected.

A SPLIT PERSONALITY?   John Jay's five papers are of little importance and will not be considered here. The bulk of *The Federalist* was written by Alexander Hamilton and James Madison. Can it be said that two authors, writing collaboratively, are able to produce a single theory? This was the case with Marx and Engels, and yet it was clearly Marx who provided the inspiration. While Engels was a man of great talent, he accepted his master's theoretical framework in all important particulars. Hamilton and Madison were men with minds of their own, and they did not agree on all subjects. While in large measure they concurred in their assumptions concerning human nature and the social structure, they parted company when it came to saying what ought to be the respective roles of the state and the individual in the good society. Hamilton's main theme was that the national government should be strong and authoritative; he cared little for the rights of the states and he was surprisingly unconcerned about the liberties of individuals. In his theoretical scheme, national power was at the center of things. With Madison, the emphasis was much more on the representation of local sentiment and the protection of citizens' rights. For him individual freedom was of central importance. On this basis it has been argued that *The Federalist* is actually a "split personality," that there are two theories on its pages rather than one.

The real answer is more complicated. Hamilton knew his own mind, and his own theory is both forceful and internally consistent. Madison, on the other hand, tended to waver between agreement with Hamilton's emphasis on national power and his own preoccupation with individual freedom. If there is a "split personality" it is to be found in Madison himself, not in *The Federalist* as a whole. This interpretation will become clear as the actual arguments of the book are set forth.

Constitutions are written for the real political world. They are not drawn up to "prove" a political theory or to impose some philosophical framework upon the citizens of a nation. The framers who met in Philadelphia were practical statesmen. If they were men of learning— and they clearly were—they put their classical educations to one side in their attempts to create a workable constitution for the new United States. At the same time, this constitution had to operate in a human and social context. Such a context is not created *by* a theory but rather develops as a product of culture and history. Nevertheless, men and societies can only be *understood* if they are viewed in the light of theory.

This the *Federalist* authors well knew, and they made clear their underlying assumptions as they propounded the arguments for the Constitution.

REALISM AND RATIONALITY

THE ATTACK ON UTOPIA Both Madison and Hamilton stressed the limited and imperfect character of human nature. There are repeated references to "ambition," "avarice," "passion," "vindictiveness," "rapacity," "rage," "resentment," "jealousy," "contention," and "irrationality" on the pages of *The Federalist.* Hamilton had the greater tendency to underscore these traits. "A man must be far gone in Utopian speculations," he wrote in No. 6, " . . . to forget that men are ambitious, vindictive, and rapacious." Even those who seem, at first glance, to adhere to the path of reason can be attacked on the grounds of harboring irrational motives. "Ambition, avarice, personal animosity, party opposition, and many other motives not more laudable than these," Hamilton wrote in No. 1, "are apt to operate as well upon those who support as those who oppose the right side of a question." From the outset the *Federalist* authors sought to establish that the proposed constitution would deal with men as they are and as they have been throughout human history. "If men were angels, no government would be necessary," Madison said in No. 51. But Americans are not angels, and while the Constitution was an instrument that would alter the structure of government, it could do nothing to change the fundamental instincts of individuals. Indeed, Hamilton was fearful that a Utopian frame of mind would work great harm on any effort to create a viable government. "Is it not time," he asked in No. 6, "to awake from the deceitful dream of a golden age and to adopt as a practical maxim for the direction of our political conduct that we, as well as other inhabitants of the globe, are yet remote from the happy empire of perfect wisdom and perfect virtue?"

To speak of the imperfect wisdom and virtue of men is to imply that there will always exist people who are ignorant and people who are perverse. At no time will all men have complete knowledge nor will there ever be universal agreement on the means and ends of public policy. The minds and behavior of citizens are continually distorted and corrupted by self-interest, and this in the face of all attempts to promote the general welfare. "As long as the reason of man continues fallible, and he is at liberty to exercise it, different opinions will be formed," Madison said in No. 10. And out of the differences of opinions will rise conflicts and tensions that must be curbed because they cannot be eradicated. The outlook of Hamilton and Madison then, was one that accepts the doctrine of original sin; there is, they assumed, a perverse streak in mankind that prevents all efforts to create a harmonious society. "Has it not invariably been found," Hamilton again asked in No. 6, "that momentary passions, and immediate interests, have a more active and impervious control over human conduct than general or remote considerations of policy, utility, or justice?" To this question both the *Federalist* authors answered an unreserved "Yes."

WHEN MEN FOREGATHER   Original sin is more than a theory of human nature. It is also a theory of group behavior. There may be some reason for believing that men, if considered singly as individuals, are potentially rational creatures and capable of altruistic behavior. For example, the writers of *The Federalist* would not have addressed their arguments to the newspaper readers of New York had they not believed in some measure that these citizens might be persuaded by the force of logic and an impressive array of arguments. However, the act of reading is highly personal; it is really a private conversation between author and reader. The implication is that human reason is most evident when the individual is isolated from his fellow citizens. But when men enter groups they become part of an atmosphere that tends to undermine whatever rational qualities its members might have possessed as individuals. This theory is especially relevant in politics, because legislative assemblies are common institutions of government. "Are not popular assemblies frequently subject to the impulses of rage, resentment, jealousy, avarice, and of other irregular and violent propensities?" Hamilton asked in No. 6. This was a rhetorical question, but if he needed an answer it was supplied by Madison in No. 38:

> The history of almost all the great councils and consultations held among mankind for reconciling their discordant opinions, assuaging their mutual jealousies and adjusting their respective interests, is a history of factions, contentions, and disappointments, and may be classed among the most dark and degraded pictures which display the infirmities and depravities of the human character.

While the legislative branch of government would have the authority to make a nation's laws, it must itself be subject to controls so that the assembled passions of its members are held in check. The difference between a legislature and a street-corner mob is one of degree. Both display the irrationalities that arise when men meet and act collectively.

LIMITING POWER

Human perversity and the clash of interests pervade the social scene. Men are creatures who cannot be trusted, and groups stand in need of external controls. It follows that the function of government is to provide a groundwork of order. For without order there can be no serious talk of liberty or equality or justice. The proposed constitution, a 7,000-word document laying down the form the new government was to take, was itself testimony that political behavior could not be left to chance. If the Constitution had a purpose it was to specify who was to possess governmental power and under what circumstances that exercise of power might be deemed legitimate. If such a document did not exist as the supreme law of the land, then the country would be left with only the hope that wise rulers might appear on the scene and that they would reconcile human differences and govern society rationally. The likelihood of the emergence of philosopher-kings, though noble as a theory, could not form a practical basis for the strife-torn America that confronted the *Federalist* authors. "It is vain to say that enlightened statesmen will be able to adjust these clashing interests and render them all subservient to the public good," Madison said in No. 10. "Enlightened statesmen will not always be at the helm." What was needed was a concrete constitutional document, a legal instrument which would be the supreme law of the land, that would provide in a specific way what was to be the allocation of power.

The theory of original sin as interpreted by Hamilton and Madison extended not only to the general citizenry and members of legislative assemblies, but to all who might hold governmental office. Their axiom, quite candidly put, was that no one was to be trusted. However, they saw ways and means for dealing with this situation. The framers of the proposed constitution began by providing for the dispersion of power into three branches of government. Hamilton described this principle in No. 9:

The science of politics, however, like most other sciences, has received great improvement. The efficacy of various principles is now well understood, which were either not known at all, or imperfectly known to the ancients. The regular distribution of power into distinct departments . . . are means, and powerful means, by which the excellencies of republican government may be retained and its imperfections lessened or avoided.

A new government that wishes to disperse power usually finds it appropriate to draw up a constitutional document specifying which institutions are permitted to perform which functions. An established society, such as Great Britain, may develop such procedures over a long period of time and without a written constitution. However, the American states had not had several centuries during which they could experiment by trial and error. They were confronted with immediate problems calling for an immediate solution.

THE SEPARATION OF POWERS   The new national government would not, then, be a monolithic structure. Hamilton and Madison both emphasized that the proposed constitution made explicit provision for three separate departments. If such a trifurcation was not the most conducive to efficiency, it was nevertheless necessary if the freedoms of citizens and the identities of states were to be protected. "No political truth is certainly of greater intrinsic value, or is stamped with the authority of more enlightened patrons of liberty," Madison wrote in No. 47, "than that . . . the accumulation of all powers, legislative, executive, and judiciary, in the same hands, whether of one, a few, or many, and whether hereditary, self-appointed, or elective, may justly be pronounced the very definition of tyranny."

The idea that powers can be separated is a principle of government rather than an explicit guide to practice. Indeed, three different interpretations can be given to the separation-of-powers theory.

1. Separation of powers means, first of all, that a single individual will not serve in more than one branch of the government at any given time. The theory is that one set of *men* will administer the laws, and that another set of men will enact them. A legislator, for example, should not be able to ascend to the judicial bench to interpret a statute that he earlier participated in drafting. (But even the proposed constitution had at least one exception to this rule: the Vice President, a member of the

executive branch, would preside over the Senate and would have a vote there in case of a tie.)

2. The next meaning of separation of powers is that the legislative, executive, and judicial *functions* are different and that they should be performed by the three independent branches. Making laws, administering laws, and interpreting laws are separate processes and whatever overlap there is among them can and should be held to a minimum. The Constitution, for example, forbade the Congress from passing bills of attainder; for the punishment of individual citizens is a judicial function.

3. And, finally, the principle goes on to assert that each branch should have some *check* over the operations of the others. The jurisdiction of any one department must be sufficiently broad so that it can, as occasion demands, veto the acts of its coequal departments. Such a veto need not be permanent or final, and it need not be applicable in all circumstances. Sometimes it will serve as a delaying action, forcing a department to reconsider the wisdom of a measure it may have enacted in haste. At other times a veto will be a potential weapon and thus one branch will, in fear or anticipation, temper its behavior lest it be checked by another. Indeed, the potentiality of checks and balances probably has more day-to-day effectiveness than their actual use. For politicians have a tendency to anticipate sanctions and thus act in ways that will make the actual employment of those sanctions unnecessary.

The theory of mutual checks and balances can best be understood if one visualizes a triangle with six arrows skirting its three borders, as shown on the diagram. Each arrow represents the one or more checks that one branch has over another. Some of these checks come readily to mind: the President's veto of acts of Congress, congressional approval of executive appointees, the Supreme Court's review of administration rules and regulations. Others are less obvious: congressional modification and repassage of a law to circumvent a Supreme Court decision; or the President's refusal to spend money that Congress has appropriated for a particular purpose. A student of American government should be able to "fill in the arrows" in some detail and be able to describe the wide variety of checks that are available to the various departments. At the same time he must understand that some are more important than others, that some are used frequently and others hardly at all.

The theory of mutual checks and balances

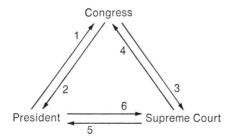

PARCHMENT AND PRACTICE Madison was quick to admit that any application of the principle of separation of powers would be beset with practical difficulties. In No. 37 he acknowledged that the science of politics has yet to find a way of encasing men and functions in airtight compartments:

> Experience has instructed us that no skill in the science of government has yet been able to discriminate and define, with sufficient certainty, its three great provinces—the legislative, executive, and judiciary; or even the privileges and powers of the different legislative branches. Questions daily occur in the course of practice which prove the obscurity which reigns in these subjects, and which puzzle the greatest adepts in political science.

Indeed, the whole notion of dispersing power among several governmental departments did not come from any treatise in political theory, but was rather derived from the political experience of the states and before them the colonies. From Georgia to New Hampshire, from the time of the establishment of the earliest colonial legislature, there had been various attempts to separate the major functions of government into discrete agencies. Yet none of the states or colonies provided a perfect illustration of the principle. In No. 47 Madison surveyed the experience of all 13 states and concluded: "There is not a single instance in which the several departments of power have been kept absolutely separate and distinct."

A written constitution had to operate within practical considerations. The separation of powers, accompanied by checks and balances, would be written into the basic law as a curb on the national government. But that in itself would not be enough. "A mere demarcation on parchment of the constitutional limits of the several departments," Madison said in No. 48, "is not a sufficient guard against those encroachments which lead to a tyrannical concentration of all the powers of government in the same hands." Other extraconstitutional protections—in No. 51 he called them "auxiliary precautions"—would be needed. And these, as will be seen, would be found not in a parchment document but in the very fabric of American society itself.

A REPRESENTATIVE CONSTITUTION

A DEMOCRACY OR A REPUBLIC?   To the minds of the *Federalist* authors, democracy was something to be feared. For to them it conveyed the idea of direct self-government on the part of the people. In its least objectionable form, it would mean local government by a town meeting where the whole adult population of a community would participate in making policy. At the other extreme, it would involve enacting national legislation by popular referendum. The *Federalist* authors' distrust of democracy was based on their theory of human nature. For if citizens are fundamentally intemperate and irrational, especially when they assemble, then the laws they enact will corrupt the true ends of government. For Hamilton and Madison, then, "democracy" was construed as "popular democracy," even "populist democracy."

Although the town meeting has ceased to be an important institution, and referendums are confined to the state and local levels, the *Federalist* conception of democracy continues to have relevance in American politics. What it connotes, in essence, is an attitude of mind on the part of ordinary citizens. The people in a popular democracy will continually be preoccupied with governmental policy and will form and express their opinions without stopping to ask if they have the competence to do so. Elected officeholders, under such circumstances, will be forced to heed the whims of their constituents or else suffer defeat at the next election. Democratic citizens, then, do not simply elect their rulers. What characterizes the citizens of a popular democracy is that *between* elections they continue to voice their political sentiments and exert an undue influence over the men and women they placed in public office. While this conception of democracy may be a caricature, it must be remembered that fear gives rise to a gross exaggeration of reality. And Hamilton and Madison were haunted by the fear of a public that would be overinterested in the affairs of government, obtrusive in their behavior, and arrogant in their demeanor.

THE DEFERENTIAL VOTER The proposed constitution, therefore, was not intended to be a democratic instrument. Citizens were to have the vote, but once Election Day was over the business of government was to remain in the hands of the elected representatives. This "republican" —as opposed to "democratic"—arrangement, Madison wrote in No. 10, was designed "to refine and enlarge the public views by passing them through the medium of a chosen body of citizens, whose wisdom may best discern the true interest of their country and whose patriotism and love of justice will be least likely to sacrifice it to temporary or partial considerations." This suggests that there do exist in society at least *some* men who are superior to others in regard to wisdom, patriotism, and love of justice. For all their generalizations about the parlous state of the human condition, Hamilton and Madison nevertheless relied heavily on the expectation that men of superior qualities would rise to positions of power in the governmental system.

How was this to occur? The *Federalist* authors adhered to the hope that the average voter would, when elections were held, defer to men of greater attainments than his own. Rather than looking for a candidate coming from his own class or occupation, the ordinary citizen would vote for someone he acknowledged to be his better. In No. 35 Hamilton asserted that "mechanics and manufacturers"—which at that time referred to skilled and unskilled workers—would have the good sense to elect businessmen rather than people from their own station in life:

Mechanics and manufacturers will always be inclined, with few exceptions, to give their votes to merchants in preference to persons of their own professions or trades. Those discerning citizens are well aware . . . that the merchant is their natural patron and friend; and they are aware that however great the confidence they may justly feel in their own good sense, their interests can be more effectually promoted by the merchant than by themselves. They are sensible that their habits in life have not been such as to give them those acquired endowments, without which in a deliberative assembly the greatest natural abilities are for the most part useless.

Whether this statement is a prediction of what *would* in fact happen or an expression of a hope concerning what *ought* to happen is difficult to say. In one sense, Hamilton was suggesting that the ordinary voters would defer to citizens of superior attainments. In another, there is the impression that Hamilton was exhorting the skilled and unskilled workers among his readers to exhibit some humility in their voting behavior and to display a measure of deference when they went to the polls.

THE DEFERENTIAL CANDIDATE   Habits of deference would have to be engendered if the republican principle was to be established. On the one hand, rulers were to be elected either directly or indirectly, and it was hoped that they would be the most capable men in society. "The aim of every political constitution is, or ought to be, first to obtain for rulers men who possess most wisdom to discern, and most virtue to pursue, the common good of the society," Madison said in No. 57. And then later on the same page he stated that the franchise, the instrument for deciding who will govern, will be universally extended:

> Who are to be the electors of [i.e., voters for] the federal representatives? Not the rich, more than the poor; not the learned, more than the ignorant; not the haughty heirs of distinguished names, more than the humble sons of obscurity and unpropitious fortune. The electors are to be the great body of the people of the United States.

Hamilton and Madison believed that universality of suffrage and superiority of representation could be reconciled if the elected lawmakers took pains to keep in touch with the needs of their constituents. While a legislator might not come from the same class as the people in his district, he could nevertheless acquaint himself with their sentiments and interests. "Is it not natural that a man who is a candidate for the favor of the people . . . should take care to inform himself of their dispositions and inclinations and should be willing to allow them their proper degree of influence upon his conduct?" Hamilton asked in No.

35. Madison answered this question in No. 57 by pointing to the elements that would link representatives and constituents: "Duty, gratitude, interest, ambition itself, are the cords by which they will be bound to fidelity and sympathy with the great mass of the people." It is interesting to note how certain themes recur in this analysis. Hamilton took pains to point out that voters should exert no more than their "proper degree of influence" upon their representatives, that they should forbear from interfering in affairs that are best left to those who are able to take a long-range view. And Madison went on to state that while elected lawmakers may be superior men, they also possess the less praiseworthy qualities of interest and ambition, and these would help keep them attentive to the needs of those with the power to elect them to office. In this way, then, the republican basis of a "parchment constitution" is underpinned by traits of human behavior which might otherwise pursue less noble purposes. In other words, a system of government must not try to abolish interests and emotions but must rather channel them so that they serve the national welfare.

THE PURPOSES OF POLITICS

POWER: NATIONAL AND INTERNATIONAL The assumption of the *Federalist* authors was that before self-government is possible it is necessary to have a government, that political authority must be established before individual liberty can be secured. This is why *The Federalist* does not constitute a treatise on democracy; it is why it always discusses freedom in the context of social order. The men who drafted the proposed constitution were persuaded that the national government needed to be strong, and this conviction was founded on real fears. There was not only the threat of conflict between the states but also of insurrection within the states. The memory of Shays' Rebellion in Massachusetts was still fresh; and the tensions between states over title to what were then considered western lands were causes for concern. The specter of European power rose across the Atlantic, and not a few of these nations ringed the new America with their colonies in the Western Hemisphere. Added to this was the frequency of Indian wars and the intensity of commercial competition. All these were real threats and they could be checked only if national power was created to meet the challenge. "I acknowledge my aversion to every project that is calculated to disarm the government of a single weapon, which in any possible contingency might be usefully employed for the general defense and security," Hamilton wrote in No. 36.

Hamilton's concern over creating a strong nation was not a little infused with patriotism of his own. He was a proud American and it was his fervent desire to show to the countries of Europe that the new republic would more than hold its own in the arena of world affairs. In No. 11 he allowed his emotions to flow freely:

> Europe, by her arms and by her negotiations, by force and by fraud, has in different degrees extended her dominion . . . Africa, Asia, and America have successively felt her domination. The superiority she has long maintained has tempted her to plume herself as mistress of the world, and to consider the rest of mankind as created for her benefit. Men admired as profound philosophers have in direct terms attributed to her inhabitants a physical superiority and have gravely asserted that all animals, and with them the human species, degenerate in America—that even dogs cease to bark after having breathed awhile in our atmosphere. Facts have too long supported these arrogant pretensions of the European. It belongs to us to vindicate the honor of the human race, and to teach that assuming brother moderation. Union will enable us to do it. Disunion will add another victim to his triumphs. Let Americans disdain to be the instruments of European greatness!

The emotion of national pride invariably accompanies political realism as a new country seeks to establish itself. The patronizing manner of the Europeans rankled American sensibilities; Hamilton sought to show that the United States could stand up against England, France, and Spain if it were prepared to create a central government having the power to act purposively.

Yet the emphasis was not solely on military strength. National power, to Hamilton's mind, must be used to create a viable economy. Commerce and industry had to be encouraged; and a stable business community for both domestic and foreign investors had to be maintained. The mercantile acts that Britain had imposed on the colonies stifled economic growth. It was Hamilton's vision that it was the responsibility of government to give capitalism every possible stimulus; and later, as Secretary of the Treasury, he proposed a wide variety of policies to encourage the emerging entrepreneurs. "Under a vigorous national government," he said in No. 11, "the natural strength and resources of the country, directed to a common interest, would baffle all the combinations of European jealousy to restrain our growth." But governmental support of trade and manufacturing was not simply designed to tweak the nose of Europe. On the contrary, Hamilton continued, "an active commerce, an extensive navigation, and a flourishing marine would then be the inevitable offspring of moral and physical necessity." The positive purpose was to build a nation by encouraging an industrialized economy. American capitalism would develop only if a vigorous government gave its authoritative support to the business community. In putting this idea forward, Hamilton was not only foreseeing the future; he was also serving to shape the subsequent centuries of American life.

Turning to the domestic scene, Hamilton saw no less reason for securing national power. While others might talk of the importance of individual freedom, minority rights, and local autonomy, Hamilton spoke of the threats from factionalism, rebellion, and license. To him the several states were so many seedbeds of disruption and disorder. Had not Shays' uprising in Massachusetts been but the latest of many recent challenges to authority? If Europe was to be kept at bay and if productive property was to be safeguarded at home, then national political authority had to be centralized. To drive home this lesson, Hamilton cited the experience of history, and warned his readers that what had happened in the past could well occur again. In No. 9 he wrote:

> A firm union will be of the utmost moment to the peace and liberty of the states as a barrier against domestic faction and insurrection. It is impossible to read the history of the petty republics of Greece and Italy without feeling sensations of horror and disgust at the distractions with which they were continually agitated, and at the rapid succession of revolutions by which they were kept in a state of perpetual vibration between the extremes of tyranny and anarchy.

If events made it necessary, governmental power might even deploy itself by marching into a state or locality to put down those citizens who refused to obey national law. Hamilton was later to use national power in just that way, to deal with the Whisky Rebellion in Pennsylvania, for it was clear to him that political authority was meaningless if it did not have the ability to compel.

MADISON'S DILEMMA In this part of the discussion, Madison tended to remain silent. This was not because he disagreed with his coauthor but was rather due to desire to reconcile opposing political principles. Madison, too, was worried about domestic factionalism, and he knew full well that conflicting interests could damage the public well-being as they pursued their self-centered ends. "The regulation of these various and interfering interests forms the principal task of modern legislation," he said in No. 10; and the exercise of such regulation "involves the spirit of party and faction in the necessary and ordinary operations of the government." But Madison, as will be seen shortly, wanted it both ways. If he acknowledged that political power must be used to regulate the activities of groups in the society, he also wanted those groups to play a positive role in making governmental policy. In other words, groups must not only be regulated—they must also be represented in the government of the republic. In No. 37, he reminded his readers that such a reconciliation had been intended by the men who drew up the Constitution. "Among the difficulties encountered by the convention," he said, "a very important one must have lain in combining the requisite stability and energy in government with the inviolable attention due to liberty and the republican form."

The tensions between authority and liberty, between regulation and representation, are continually present. Hamilton was most concerned to effect the consolidation of national power as a first step, and he was often impatient with those who demanded guarantees of freedom against an allegedly oppressive government. At the same time, he wanted to protect the liberty of at least one group in society—its businessmen—and he proposed that public agencies bend every effort to assist those engaged in developing the economy. As for individuals lacking in wealth or ambition—which is to say the majority of Americans—Hamilton was distinctly unimpressed with whatever claims they might make for political attention. Indeed, he suspected that accommodating majority sentiment would jeopardize the freedoms of the minority that really counted. The politician who takes seriously the whims and wishes of the general public is a dangerous man. "Of those men who have overturned the liberties of republics," he wrote in No. 1, "the greatest number have begun their careers by paying obsequious court to the people, commencing demagogues and ending tyrants."

Madison was never so harsh when he spoke of the common man and he was slower to denigrate popular leaders. Nevertheless, he too was a republican rather than a democrat, according to his understanding of those terms, and he was wary of untempered majority rule. Where he parted company with Hamilton was in his solutions to problems that the two men agreed had to be solved. Whereas Hamilton stressed the vigorous use of national power, Madison reemphasized constitutional checks. One reason for this difference in approach may be suggested. Both *Federalist* authors wanted America to be a free society. However, the question arises: Freedom for whom? Hamilton wanted to protect the freedom of businessmen and others who would contribute to the growth of the nation's economy. This group, he felt, must be safeguarded from tyranny at the hands of a jealous and underprivileged majority. Madison, on the other hand, wanted to guarantee the rights of a rather different minority. He was concerned about freedom of expression: the liberty to speak, assemble, and worship as one pleased. And constitutional provisions would not suffice as a defense of these freedoms. Something more was needed, and therefore Madison looked to the basic structure of American society for his answer.

REVIEW QUESTIONS

1. What is the *Federalist* theory of human nature?
2. What is the value of basing a government on a written constitution?
3. What is the separation of powers designed to achieve?
4. Why did the *Federalist* authors fear democracy?
5. In what spheres did Hamilton advocate a strenuous government?
6. Did Madison accept Hamilton's ideas on national power?

6 FEDERAL GOVERNMENT AND SOCIAL PLURALISM

The thirteen states, as British colonies, all had separate identities for many years prior to the Revolution. They were, therefore, communities in their own right and each had a history and a local pride of its own. In order to secure even rudimentary agreement on the proposed constitution, the *Federalist* authors had to persuade their readers that all the states would retain significant power in local matters. Hamilton and Madison were well aware of the strength of the opposition to the Constitution. In No. 1, Hamilton frankly acknowledged that certain interests in the states would be affected by the creation of a national government. "Among the most formidable of the obstacles which the new constitution will have to encounter," he wrote, "may readily be distinguished the obvious interest of a certain class of men in every state to resist all changes which may hazard a diminution of power, emolument, and consequence of the offices they hold under the state establishments." Not simply officeholders, but hundreds of thousands of ordinary citizens with strong loyalties to the states had to be convinced that their freedoms would not be abridged. This task of persuasion fell to Madison.

In seven papers, beginning with No. 39, Madison sought to demonstrate that political power in America would be divided between the state and national governments, and that the authority granted to the national government was the minimum necessary for America's survival. Madison continually alluded to the doctrine of constitutionalism, for only with a written document would the limits on national power be demarcated and the extent of state powers be guaranteed. In other words, a federal system is possible only if the bounds of the national and state jurisdictions are specified by constitutional provisions. Without such an aid there would be constant quarrels—not only about substantive issues of power and policy but also about which agencies were legitimately entitled to settle those quarrels. Madison sought to satisfy both the proponents of centralization and states' rights by taking a middle road. In No. 39 he said: "The proposed constitution, therefore, is, in strictness, neither a national nor a federal constitution, but a composition of both."

The chief worry of the states' rights advocates was that the power granted to the national government would be used to tyrannize the various regions and localities throughout the country. Local customs and regional interests might be ignored and even injured if political authority gravitated to the center. The principle of federalism, therefore, was created to ensure that substantial power would remain in the separate states. And to this was added the principle of separation of powers, in an attempt to ensure that even the national government itself would not be monolithic in structure.

It is clear that the states' rights proponents were not the only ones who were anxious about centralized power. Even those sympathetic to the idea of national authority were concerned lest the legislative and perhaps other branches of the new government be captured by the wrong people. There was, in short, the fear of majority tyranny: the fear that with universal suffrage and widespread political participation the masses would take over and endanger the interests of vulnerable individuals in society. Madison sought to allay these anxieties, and in the course of doing this he found it necessary to present a full-scale analysis of the social structure that would underpin the American political system.

CLASSES, INTERESTS, PARTIES

American society, Madison said in No. 10, had been and would continue to be diversified and heterogeneous. The larger the collection of individuals, the more will one encounter dissimilar drives, talents, and ambitions. Variations in intelligence, energy, and aspiration can be observed among the members of a population. And this variety brings in its wake important social and psychological consequences. To begin with, a large number of interests will emerge in the society, and these will result in differences of opinion on the parts of individuals who hold them. Because the reason of man is an imperfect instrument, citizens tend to be myopic, wrongly perceiving their own interests as identical with the common good. As each person is anxious to promote his own well-being, the political opinions in society are distorted in their perception of reality and divisive in their impact. Of all the interests that blind the intelligence and promote conflict, Madison said, property is the most important. On this basis Madison links his theory of human nature with a theory of society:

> As long as the reason of man continues fallible, and he is at liberty to exercise it, different opinions will be formed. As long as the connection subsists between his reason and his self-love, his opinions and his passions will have a reciprocal influence on each other; and the former will be objects to which the latter will attach themselves. The diversity in the faculties of men, from which the rights of property originate, is not less an insuperable obstacle to the uniformity of interests. The protection of these faculties is the first object of government. From the protection of different and unequal faculties of acquiring property, the possession of different degrees and kinds of property immediately results; and from the influence of these on the sentiments and views of the respective proprietors ensues a division of the society into different interests and parties.

This passage, like all the passages in No. 10, calls for close reading. Madison is saying that human potentialities must be given the opportunity to express themselves, and that the responsibility of government in a free society is to encourage such expression. Yet if government carries out this obligation, then vigorous and talented individuals will inevitably acquire property and develop interests of their own. The possession of these interests will obscure their perception of the common good and distort their political opinions. In other words, by encouraging self-expression and property ownership the government also encourages social disharmony and human irrationality. If individual development and material success are blessings worth having, it must also be understood that they are to be had at a cost. Society will be less harmonious and the opinions and behavior of individuals will be less realistic. Madison settled for this outcome, knowing it was the price to be paid for individualism.

POWER AND PROPERTY American society, then, would be composed of many interests and groups. All of them would pursue goals of their own; and none of them, despite their protestations to the contrary, would promote the general welfare. These groups—Madison called them "factions"—present a challenge to government because they accentuate whatever differences there are in society and they necessarily compete for power with their own interests in mind. Again in No. 10, Madison elaborated his theory and it deserves to be quoted in full:

> The latent causes of faction are thus sown in the nature of man; and we see them everywhere brought into different degrees of activity, according to the different circumstances of civil society. A zeal for different opinions concerning religion, concerning government, and many other points, as well of speculation as of practice; an attachment to different leaders ambitiously contending for pre-eminence and power; or to persons of other descriptions whose fortunes have been interesting to the human passions, have, in turn, divided mankind into parties, inflamed them with mutual animosity, and rendered them much more disposed to vex and oppress each other than to co-operate for their common good.
>
> So strong is this propensity of mankind to fall into mutual animosities that where no substantial occasion presents itself the most frivolous and fanciful distinctions have been sufficient to kindle their unfriendly passions and excite their most violent conflicts.
>
> But the most common and durable source of factions has been the various and unequal distribution of property. Those who hold and those who are without property have ever formed distinct interests in society. Those who are creditors and those who are debtors, fall under a like discrimination. A

landed interest, a manufacturing interest, a mercantile interest, a moneyed interest, with many lesser interests, grow up of necessity in civilized nations, and divide them into different classes, actuated by different sentiments and views.

The regulation of these various and interfering interests forms the principal task of modern legislation and involves the spirit of party and faction in the necessary and ordinary operations of the government.

VERTICAL VERSUS HORIZONTAL INTERESTS The "most common and durable" source of division in society, Madison said, must be attributed to property ownership. The propertied and the propertyless classes are the two most significant groups, and any analysis of social conflict must begin with the tensions between them. However, Madison's framework does not end at this point. In addition to these two main classes, there are many interests in society. Madison's meaning may best be understood by contrasting a "horizontal" division, representing the propertied and propertyless classes, against the various "vertical" divisions, representing the disparate interests within the two major classes.

The diagram shows that where there is a division *between* the propertied and propertyless classes, there are also subdivisions—and hence disagreements—*within* the two classes. Property owners who are creditors will often be in conflict with property owners who are debtors; manufacturers will not always agree with financiers. At the same time, there will frequently be a sense of fellow feeling among the members of the two classes *within* an interest. Thus, while the propertyless class is in the majority, the people who comprise it are by no means single-minded in their interests.

This depiction of society lessens the possibility that the propertyless majority will use its power to tyrannize those who own property. As Hamilton pointed out in his discussion of voting behavior, there is reason to believe that individuals employed in farming or commerce or manufacturing will identify their own interests with those of their employers and will allow members of the propertied class to represent them. Thus, both the bank owner and the bank clerk, one a man of property and the other not, belong to the "financial interest" and will often stand together against competing interests.

Furthermore, while Madison granted that property might be the most common and durable source of political division, he also pointed out that

Classes and interests

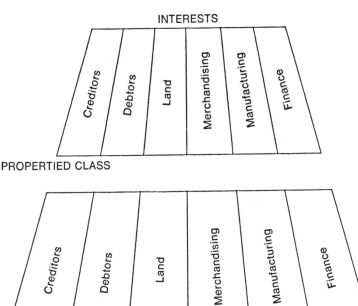

PROPERTIED CLASS

PROPERTYLESS CLASS

"many lesser interests" grow up. And by these he clearly meant religious interests, ethnic interests, regional interests, and ideological interests. While these, to his mind, might be of lesser importance they did play a role in politics and often a key one. Finally, Madison saw it as government's role to regulate interests as well as to represent them. The state, for Madison, was to stand apart from and serve as a control over the activities of interests and groups. This meant that the government would have a source of power and goals that were independent of any one class or interest.

THE SIZE OF SOCIETY   The thirteen states had a population of approximately 3 million, and in terms of numbers alone it was clear that the United States would be a large country. To the members of minority groups who worried about possible majority tyranny under the proposed constitution, Madison pointed out that the very size of the new nation would go far toward dampening this threat. "The greater number of citizens and extent of territory," he said in No. 10, will be the "circumstance principally which renders factious combinations less to be dreaded." There might be great hordes of propertyless workers in Massachusetts and New York; but as individuals they would also have diverse regional, occupational, and religious loyalties and it seemed highly unlikely that they would combine across state boundaries to organize a single "working-class" party.

This is why Madison favored a nation that would cover a large territory. "Extend the sphere and you take in a greater variety of parties and interests," he continued in No. 10. "You make it less probable that a majority of the whole will have a common motive to invade the rights of other citizens." A further consequence would be to localize any tendency toward majority tyranny. If the propertyless class ascended to power in, say, Georgia or Pennsylvania, it would be improbable that such a revolution would contaminate neighboring states or the country as a whole. Madison concluded No. 10 by predicting that "the influence of factious leaders may kindle a flame within their particular states but will be unable to spread a general conflagration through the other states."

POLITICS WITHOUT PARTIES   Neither Hamilton nor Madison approved of political parties. Factions, classes, and interests were seen as the necessary accompaniments of a free society; but they were a challenge rather than a blessing. If political groupings were to be based on property or other interests, it was to be hoped that they would confine their activities to localities and to promoting specific policies rather than comprehensive programs. The idea that factions might organize as political parties and run candidates for public office was something that the *Federalist* authors preferred not to consider. To their minds there was sufficient disharmony in society without institutionalizing those tensions in the political system. As far as Hamilton and Madison could see, individual candidates would present themselves for election; there would be no party labels and no slates of nominees. In this way, voters would cast their ballots in their role as *citizens* rather than on the basis of special interests they might have. Furthermore, candidates would be judged on their merits and they would have to make a broad appeal to a large and diversified electorate in their constituencies. Above all, the *Federalist* authors wanted to avoid national parties—parties that would coalesce the interests within various states into centralized organizations. For all their concern to establish a national government, they were unwilling to espouse parties conceived on similar lines. The reason for this was that Hamilton and Madison, no less than many of their readers, were fearful of the rise of a majority party that would trample on the rights and liberties of minorities. "When a majority is included in a faction," Madison wrote in No. 10, "the form of popular government . . . enables it to sacrifice to its ruling passion or interest both the public good and the rights of their citizens." National parties, especially if one of them attracted a majority to its banner, would do much to bring about just this result.

THE SOCIOLOGY OF FREEDOM

In No. 51, Madison continued to relate his theories of human nature and social structure to his view of political liberty. In permitting universal suffrage and representative institutions, the framers of the Constitution granted that government was to be based on the consent of the governed. This meant that politics would be a reflection of society, that the interests and aspirations of social interests and classes would contribute to shaping the political system. It was for that reason that Madison, in No. 10, devoted so much attention to his sociological analysis. With this task accomplished, he was ready to turn to the problem of human freedom. How can the rights of minorities be reconciled with majority rule? To speak thus of "majority rule" is to make the assumption that a permanent and homogeneous "majority" will emerge to monopolize political power. On the contrary, Madison asserted in No. 51, there is reason to believe that this will not be the path of development in America:

> Whilst all authority in it will be derived from and dependent on the society, the society itself will be broken into so many parts, interests and classes of citizens, that the rights of individuals, or of the minority, will be in little danger from interested combinations of the majority. In a free government the security for civil rights must be the same as that for religious rights. It consists in the one case in the multiplicity of interests, and in the other in the

multiplicity of sects. The degree of security in both cases will depend on the number of interests and sects; and this may be presumed to depend on the extent of country and number of people comprehended under the same government.

The American "majority," in other words, will be a shifting coalition of groups. Its composition, in terms of the people who belong to it, will alter from time to time and from issue to issue. A citizen may find himself on the majority side one day but on the next he will be among the dissenters. While part of the time every individual may have to abide by majority dictates he finds disagreeable, there is little likelihood that the members of any one group in society will suffer sustained and uninterrupted oppression.

INTERESTS: INDIVIDUAL AND SOCIAL The "multiplicity of interests" that Madison spoke of must be construed at two levels: the individual and the social. In the former instance, each citizen will himself have several interests he wishes to promote. In the latter instance, society as a whole will be composed of various interests, each attracting the loyalties of groups of citizens.

On the individual level, it can be suggested that each American will have a religious interest, an occupational interest, and various others. One citizen might, for example, be (1) a bank employee, (2) a Methodist, (3) a suburbanite, (4) a member of the white race, and also (5) an opera lover. In all five of these "roles" he will have political opinions, ranging from government regulation of banking to public subsidies for opera. In some of his roles, as when he is white and a Protestant, he will be in the American majority. Such a citizen, therefore, will sometimes belong to the majority and sometimes to a minority, depending on the issues involved. In his majority role as a white man, he may be indifferent to the needs of nonwhites who comprise a minority in the community. In his own minority role as an opera lover, he may feel his interests unappreciated by the majority, who prefer television comedies and do not want to pay taxes to support Wagner or Mozart. Madison's assumption, then, was that all Americans would possess a variety of interests, both economic and noneconomic, and that they would consequently play several roles in the political drama. Were citizens to have but a single interest, and were that interest to concern the presence or absence of property ownership, then there would indeed be the danger of a minority being continually victimized in the society.

In terms of society, Madison said that the social whole would be "broken into so many parts, interests, and classes of citizens." No single part or interest or class would contain a majority of citizens; if a majority were formed on any issue, it would simply consist of a transient coalition of groups. For example, there is a Protestant majority in America, and it may be inquired why its representatives do not enact legislation penalizing the Catholic minority in the country. Madison's answer was not that the Protestants are notably tolerant nor was it that they believe in religious liberty for all. The answer was that the Protestant majority is itself a coalition of Baptists, Methodists, Episcopalians, Presbyterians, and Lutherans. Each of these denominations had had its own history of persecution when it was in the minority, and therefore all of them agree to tolerate other religions—including Catholics—for fear that they may at some future time be subjected to majority oppression. Furthermore, not all members of the Protestant coalition believe that Catholics ought to be penalized, and were that issue even to be raised there would be every chance that the Protestant coalition would fall apart. In a pluralistic society, toleration becomes the operative rule in the political game. Respect for the freedom of others is the price paid for having one's own freedom left intact. Political liberty is guaranteed not so much by a constitution—which is, after all, a "demarcation on parchment"—as it is a product of the toleration that groups impose on themselves.

CONFLICT AND THE GENERAL GOOD   Madison ended No. 51 by assuring his readers that majority tyranny lay more in their imaginations than in the American reality:

> In the extended republic of the United States, and among the great variety of interests, parties, and sects which it embraces, a coalition of a majority of the whole society could seldom take place on any other principles than those of justice and the general good; whilst there being thus less danger to a minority from the will of a major party, there must be less pretext, also, to provide for the security of the former, by introducing into the government a will not dependent on the latter, or, in other words, a will independent of the society itself.

The kinds of policies that will muster the support of coalition-type majorities will, in all likelihood, promote the public welfare.

On first reading, this proposition of Madison's runs directly counter to Hamilton's view, stated in No. 6, that "momentary passions and immediate interests have a more active and imperious control over human conduct than general or remote considerations of policy, utility, or justice." How does one square the *Federalist* conception of human nature, as expressed by Hamilton, with Madison's contention that justice and political freedom may ultimately be secured via the group struggle? The answer is that these ends are achieved not *because* of human nature but *in spite of* it. Individuals and groups are passionate and self-interested, Madison would certainly grant, but out of their clashes in the political arena must emerge compromises. Freedom and justice are not attained because rational men consciously pursue those goals. Human reason is too imperfect and human perversity is too pervasive to allow for that. On the contrary, the public good is an unanticipated by-product of group conflict; the general welfare develops out of the collisions of particular interests and it is expressed in compromises where all parties are partially satisfied but where none are entirely contented.

Madison seemed to prefer having a "neutral" government, for he was uneasy about the creation of "a will independent of the society itself." He was concerned lest political authority become a power apart from the individuals and groups who comprise the society. For history had amply demonstrated that agencies of government are apt to fall into the hands of individuals prone to use them to promote interests detrimental to the general welfare. A government having a will of its own, a government that is impervious to the needs of the interests that make up society, can be just as tyrannical as one based on popular consent.

Yet Madison was not able to be entirely consistent in this area. In speaking of the group struggle, he said in No. 10, "the regulation of these various and interfering interests forms the principal task of modern legislation." Yet if government is to regulate groups in society by means of legislation, then the power behind that legislation must clearly emanate from a "will independent of society." The point, of course, is that neither principle—government as representative versus government as regulator—must be carried to an extreme. Government must be responsive to the expressed will of the people, but it must also have a will of its own. Hamilton stressed the latter case and there were times, especially in No. 10, when Madison supported him. On other occasions, particularly in No. 51, Madison expressed fears of a too strenuous government. Madison's two minds express an enduring dilemma in political life. If government is too indulgent in catering to the demands of interest groups, then it may not be able to fashion policies that will serve the interests of the nation as a whole. But a strong and purposeful government may exceed its mandate and commit the country to courses of action it will later regret. Unfortunately, it is evading the issue to say that these two outlooks should be "balanced." What must be achieved is an understanding of how the regulation of interests rather than their representation affects different groups in society. Those who fear and those who welcome governmental activity in a particular sphere usually have different conceptions of what makes for individual freedom and the good life. What appears to be "regulation" to the eyes of some groups looks like "representation" to others. Behind the argument over supposedly abstract principles, then, lies not so much a conflict of ideas as of interests. This, in sum, is the Madisonian lesson.

PROBLEMS FOR PLURALISM   Madison assumed that by virtue of their group identifications and memberships, all citizens would be represented in the making of public policy. This has certainly been true for individuals who have relatively concrete interests leading to a specific legislative focus. Businessmen, farmers, and many professional people know just what they want from government, and they have the resources to exert influence in an effective way. Yet all in all, the pluralist arena has been occupied to best advantage by groups that are already relatively wealthy. They possess the knowledge, experience, and financial backing it takes to mount a convincing case. Certainly the poor, the aged, and others at the margins of society have not been full participants in the pluralist process. Of course, old people could organize into an association, as might prison inmates or migrant workers. But on the whole they do not, or at least not with any great success. Until or unless this happens, large numbers of Americans will find themselves having to settle for what is left over after groups with better organizations have obtained political preferment.

Another consequence of the pluralist emphasis has been to deflect attention from the class composition of American society. Indeed this was just what Madison wanted, preferring that the country fragment itself into a multitude of interest groups. One result is that salaried workers may identify their own interests with those of the industry which employs them, thus preventing as clear-cut a confrontation between labor and management as there might otherwise be. Or insofar as people look on themselves as taxpayers or homeowners, they often oppose costly governmental programs even though such outlays may enhance the long-term welfare of the nation. The point here is not that pluralism encourages conflict, but rather that the attitudes and alliances it engenders can obscure an understanding of more deep-seated divisions in society.

Furthermore, it may well be that despite the pluralist formula the United States does in fact now contain a single majority that maintains continuing power in many important areas. For the majority of Americans belong to the white race and are moderately comfortable in economic terms. The people in this group tend to support the police, maintain a patriotic posture, and display little sympathy for radicalism, homosexuality, or other expressions they deem unsafe or subversive. The sentiments held by this majority explain, for example, the very slow pace of progress experienced by nonwhite citizens; for most Americans have nothing to gain by racial reforms, and many fear they may lose much by such measures. Similarly, the poor and other minorities requiring public support remain close to a subsistence level because the majority of voters are in no mood to grant more than minimal appropriations for welfare programs. While this majority does not belong to a single political party, its outlook receives representation in local government, state legislatures, and the Congress. The problem for black Americans, for instance, is that they will always be outvoted; therefore such attention as they receive will be largely on terms found acceptable by the white majority. The pluralist prescription breaks down when any minorities find themselves disbarred from equal participation in the arena where power must be deployed to achieve position and privilege.

THE ISOLATED DISSENTER There remains one further area where governmental power must necessarily operate independent of group power. In No. 51, Madison expressed concern for both "the rights of individuals or of the minority." However, there are many isolated individuals in society who do not belong to groups in any meaningful sense of that term, and yet who need political protection if they are to exercise their rights of expression. For example, a housewife who disapproves of the local schools and who wishes to educate her children at home; or a union member who does not want the money he pays in dues used for political purposes. These are isolated individuals, and they are not usually represented in the give-and-take of the group struggle. Their freedoms can be abridged by a private organization such as a trade union, or by a local authority like a school board, or by agencies of the national government. The rights of individuals—as distinct from groups—can be protected only if some other department of the government intervenes and exercises power on their behalf. The courts are most frequently called upon to perform this function, as the executive and legislative branches are not always sensitive to individual idiosyncrasies. When the courts so act, they do so as an arm of government and in many cases rule in defiance of majority sentiment. Whether Madison considered judicial decisions as comprising a "will independent of society" remains unclear. Perhaps he felt that his sociology of freedom was undertaking a substantial enough task in attempting to protect minority groups and that guarantees for isolated individuals would have to come from other sources.

REVIEW QUESTIONS

1. How does federalism protect freedom?

2. What are "factions" and why was Madison fearful of them?

3. Why is it important that society be broken into "many parts, interests, and classes"?

4. Is the threat of majority tyranny a real or an imaginary danger?

5. What is the role of government in relation to group conflict?

6. How are the rights of isolated individuals to be protected?

7 INSTITUTIONS OF GOVERNMENT

As they discussed the powers and functions of the major branches of the national government the *Federalist* authors were compelled to forecast how these institutions would operate in the future. Prediction, especially in the political realm, is always a risky enterprise. How can the drafters of a constitution foresee the ways in which governmental practice will develop over subsequent decades? The important point is that Hamilton and Madison made so many penetrating prophecies. To be sure, they were often wrong in their judgments; but it is too much to ask mortal men to be always correct in visualizing what will occur in the centuries subsequent to their time. Who among us can say what the government of the United States will look like in the year 2000?

THE CONGRESS

By the standards that prevailed at the time of the writing of *The Federalist,* the House of Representatives was to be a large body. Its initial membership, upon ratification of the Constitution, was to stand at 65. In contrast, there would be only 26 senators. In No. 58, Madison suggested that the House of Representatives would be more powerful than the Senate; and this would be so because the members of the House, taken together, would represent a majority of the electorate. That is, the votes that elected the representatives in each district to office would add up to a national majority, thus providing that chamber with a powerful constituency of countrywide proportions. In this connection Madison wrote in No. 58:

> Notwithstanding the equal authority which will subsist between the two houses on all legislative subjects . . . it cannot be doubted that the House, composed of the greater number of members, when supported by the more powerful states, and speaking the known and determined sense of a majority of people, will have no small advantage in a question depending on the comparative firmness of the two houses.

The House of Representatives, then, would be susceptible to democratic pressures. It would be likely to carry out the wishes of the majority of the American people without questioning the wisdom of these mandates. This would be so because Representatives would have only two-year terms and therefore have to be sensitive to the demands of their constituents if they wished to continue in office. Furthermore, the more populous states would swing substantial weight, perhaps wielding their power by means of "bloc" voting on legislation. If there was one institution in the new government that caused unease in the minds of the *Federalist* authors it was plainly the House of Representatives. As early as in No. 6 Hamilton had asked, "are not popular assemblies frequently subject to the impulses of rage, resentment, jealousy, avarice, and of other irregular and violent propensities?"

"THE IRON LAW OF OLIGARCHY"   Madison's approach was less impassioned and more analytical. With the membership of the House of Representatives to stand at 65 and with the odds that it would grow in size, there was reason to believe that it would be manipulated by an oligarchic elite. His statement of this "law," in No. 58, is as follows:

> In all legislative assemblies the greater the number composing them may be, the fewer will be the men who will in fact direct their proceedings. In the first place, the more numerous any assembly may be, of whatever characters composed, the greater is known to be the ascendancy of passion over reason. In the next place, the larger the number, 'the greater will be the proportion of members with limited information and of weak capacities. Now, it is precisely on characters of this description that the eloquence and address of the few are known to act with all their force. . . . On the same principle, the more multitudinous a representative assembly may be rendered, the more it will partake of the infirmities incident to collective meetings of the people. Ignorance will be the dupe of cunning, and passion the slave of sophistry and declamation. The people can never err more than in supposing that by multiplying their representatives beyond a certain limit they strengthen the barrier against the government of a few.

Hamilton and Madison both harbored the fear that the House of Representatives might become an indoor mob, its members listening rapt as their demogogic leaders harangued them to a fever pitch. Legislation could be enacted on impulse, based on ignorance, and productive of injustice.

What can and must be said is that the major conclusions of the *Federalist* authors may have been correct, but they were wrong in predicting the form that oligarchic rule would take in the House of Representatives. There is, indeed, an elite in the lower chamber and it certainly plays a critical role in the legislative process. But these leaders are far from being the fiery orators who stir the emotions of the rank and file. On the contrary, they are party leaders—especially the Speaker—and committee chairmen who rise to power not so much because they have extraordinary talents but rather due to their seniority. The power that accrues to them depends less on personal ambition than on the fact that decision making has to be centralized in a few hands if business is to get done at all in a large legislative chamber. The "iron law of oligarchy" foreseen by Hamilton and Madison *has* come to pass in the House of Representatives, but the oligarchs are not mob leaders. They are, on the contrary, rather ordinary men who sit at the organizational controls. The power they hold is less eye-catching than that of the demagogue, but it is more effective in the long run. Nor can these men easily be removed or replaced. For even if they were deposed, others very much like them would step into their positions.

ARISTOCRACY IN A DEMOCRACY The authors of *The Federalist* began with the assumption that original sin pervaded all of society, that all men were imperfect in reason and prone to perversity. This theory apparently applied to the rich as well as to the poor, to the educated as well as to the ignorant, to rulers as well as to the ruled. However, on at least one occasion Hamilton and Madison seemed to suggest that their strictures on human nature were not altogether universal in application. There might, in America, be some individuals who are less susceptible to irrationality and who are relatively immune to passion. Such a notion was clearly in Madison's mind when he discussed the "necessity of a well-constructed Senate" in No. 63. He wrote:

> An institution may be sometimes necessary as a defense to the people against their own temporary errors and delusions. As the cool and deliberate sense of the community ought, in all governments, and actually will, in all free governments, ultimately prevail over the views of its rulers; so there are particular moments in public affairs when the people, stimulated by some irregular passion, or some illicit advantage, or misled by the artful misrepresentations of interested men, may call for measures which they themselves will afterwards be the most ready to lament and condemn. In these critical moments, how salutary will be the interference of some temperate and respectable body of citizens, in order to check the misguided career and to suspend the blow meditated by the people against themselves, until reason, justice, and truth can regain their authority over the public mind?

In view of his prediction that the House of Representatives might be excessive and intemperate in its behavior, it was Madison's hope that the Senate would act as a counterbalance. Provisions contained in the proposed constitution made manifest this intention. Members of the upper chamber were to serve terms that were three times as long as those of their colleagues below; they were to be selected by the state legislatures rather than by popular election; and the smaller states would, in the Senate, have the power that they lacked in the House.

The people must be protected from "their own temporary errors and delusions" and the need for such protection assumes that the public does not always know its own best interests. The people, Madison's theory says, may *think* they know what they want. But in actual fact they may be blind to their *real* needs. The House of Representatives will be forced to reflect the transitory desires of its constituents. Therefore the Senate, indirectly elected and secure in its six-year terms, would be able to ignore the "errors and delusions" of the public, and correct the legislative exuberance of the House of Representatives. Madison supposed that there existed an identifiable group of "temperate and respectable" citizens and that the Senate would be recruited from this superior group. Since the time of the writing of The Federalist there has been a great deal of controversy over whether the Senate has actually checked tyrannical bills that may have been passed by the House of Representatives. It can be argued that senators, perhaps because since 1913 they have been popularly elected, are swept along by the same currents of public opinion as are the representatives. Indeed, it is not so easy as one might think to compile a list of instances where the lower chamber has acted rashly and has then been checked by its senior colleague. In addition, the "iron law of oligarchy" that operates in the House of Representatives has provided an internal set of controls not dissimilar to those exercised by the Senate.

What can be said for Madison's prediction is that senators have shown themselves to be "superior" in a number of ways when compared with members of the House of Representatives. They are less parochial because a man who aspires to the upper chamber must appeal to a broader constituency. He must have the intelligence to understand not simply one locality and one set of interests, but the habits and interests of a wide spectrum of citizens. This is particularly true at the nominating stage, when a would-be senator must make a persuasive case for his candidacy to the statewide leadership of his party. However, the "superiority" of the senators over the representatives provides not so much a hedge against tyrannical laws as an infusion of more intelligence and sophistication into the legislative process. And this end, quite obviously, is one that Hamilton and Madison fervently sought to secure.

PRESIDENT AND SUPREME COURT

The analysis of the Presidency fell to Hamilton, and to this discussion he brought the ideas that characterize his entire approach to politics. If Madison wanted a Senate composed of superior men, Hamilton was no less concerned to see the Presidency occupied by the best person America had to offer. In No. 68, he explained how the electoral college—which was to select the Chief Executive—would ensure that quality would be the uppermost consideration. The meetings of the electors in the various states would be private affairs, affording "as little opportunity as possible to tumult and disorder." The electors would meet separately at their respective state capitals and not foregather in a large and possibly discordant convention that might occur were they to make their decision collectively. All in all, the process of selecting a President would be so hedged that only the most eminent citizens would be considered, let alone chosen. Hamilton continued in No. 68:

> The process of election affords a moral certainty that the office of President will never fall to the lot of any man who is not in an eminent degree endowed with the requisite qualifications. Talents for low intrigue, the little arts of popularity, may alone suffice to elevate a man to the first honors in a single state; but it will require other talents, and a different kind of merit, to establish him in the esteem and confidence of the whole Union, or of so considerable a portion of it as would be necessary to make him a successful candidate for the distinguished office of President of the United States. It will not be too strong to say that there will be a constant probability of seeing the station filled by characters pre-eminent for ability and virtue.

When Hamilton said that a presidential candidate would have to be of sufficient stature to gain the "esteem and confidence of the whole Union," he meant not that he would be the choice of a nationwide electorate but rather of the members of the Electoral College to be appointed by the state legislatures. Since the early decades of the nineteenth century electors have felt obliged to cast their ballots for the man who has most support in the popular elections in their states. It is worth taking a moment to speculate whether the country has had fewer eminent men as President since the electors stopped using their owr judgment and began to reflect public sentiment. The change came in the

1820s, and most commentators would acknowledge that the Presidents prior to that time—Washington, Adams, Jefferson, Madison, and Monroe—presented an unbroken array of first-class talent. There have been great men in the White House since the 1820s, but there have also been incompetents and nonentities. What would have happened had the members of the electoral college continued to exercise a judgment independent of the popular vote? The answer to this question is to be found in the kind of man the state legislatures would appoint as electors. There is strong reason to believe that they would be professional politicians rather than citizens who stood "above" party, that they would be products of organization politics rather than disinterested statesmen. And considering the composition of state legislatures, the electors would tend toward a conservative or parochial posture. It is highly doubtful that they would have chosen as President an Abraham Lincoln in 1860 or a John F. Kennedy in 1960. In other words, it has been the emergence of the popular election for President—with all its "tumult and disorder"—that has given the country not a few chief executives having a national perspective. Hamilton was correct in saying that the President must be a figure who transcends regional loyalties and interests. But it was Madison who saw that the democratic process in a large nation would cancel out parochial tendencies and, by means of conference and compromise, produce leaders of stature.

AN ENERGETIC EXECUTIVE   The stress that Hamilton placed on national authority led him, quite naturally, to advocate a strong and purposive President. "Energy in the executive is a leading character in the definition of good government," he said in No. 70. And, he continued, "the ingredients which constitute energy in the executive are unity, duration, an adequate provision for its support, and competent powers." The first two of these "ingredients" are more or less self-explanatory. A unified executive means that the President is to be the sole master of his household. He must not be forced to share his authority with another agency or individual within the executive branch. So far as duration is concerned, he would have a four-year term of office and the chances were good that he could be reelected for another four years. Having one man serve eight years as Chief Executive of a country was an unusual occurrence for that time, but Hamilton realized that a powerful President would have to have an extended tenure if he were to inaugurate and implement the programs the young nation so sorely needed for its survival. The third ingredient, "adequate provision," acknowledged that the President must be suitably compensated. While he was never going to be the best-paid person in the country, he must nevertheless be financially independent so he might be relieved of personal problems and beholden to no one. George Washington's salary was $25,000 per year in 1789 and Richard Nixon's stood at $200,000 in 1972. Some of our Presidents have been wealthy men, but most have not had property holdings or private incomes of any magnitude.

But Hamilton's chief interest lay in the political powers of the President, and he devoted five papers, beginning with No. 73, to a discussion of the ways the Chief Executive could use his constitutional authority. He was to have the right to veto legislation, to serve as commander in chief, to negotiate treaties, to pardon offenders, to appoint public officials, and to address the Congress. The last power is given but cursory attention. In No. 77, Hamilton briefly mentioned the President's "giving information to Congress of the state of the Union" and his "recommending to their consideration such measures as he shall judge expedient." Yet the energetic President envisioned by Hamilton would necessarily become a legislative leader. He would have to draw up a program that was uniquely his own, and not only "recommend" it to the Congress but use all the resources of his office to see that the Senate and the House of Representatives complied with his demands. Were he simply to administer whatever laws the Congress decided that it wanted to pass, he would be little more than a glorified clerk. Hamilton's intention was made clear in No. 11, when he asserted that it was government's responsibility to promote business enterprise and to develop the nation's economy. An ambitious program like this would come only from an energetic executive. For a great deal of presidential energy would be needed to persuade a legislature dominated by rural senators and representatives who would have little sympathy for industrialization and the prospect of increased urbanization. Hamilton confined his analysis to the constitutional powers of the President and did not enter into a discussion of the practical techniques a chief executive would have to use if he wanted to secure the passage of his legislative program. But this can hardly be construed as a criticism of Hamilton. For close to two centuries, Presidents have sought to discover the most effective ways and means of becoming legislative leaders. Some have been relatively successful, others have been failures, and still others have abdicated the role completely. But none have mastered this feat in all its complexities and particulars.

GUARDIAN OF THE CONSTITUTION   Of the three branches of government, the Supreme Court received least attention in both *The Federalist* and the Constitution itself. The judicial powers of the Supreme Court were described and there was no real controversy over its authority to hear appeals from the state courts. But was the Supreme Court to have a political role as well? Here the proposed constitution was silent. While the checks and balances running from the legislature to the executive received extensive consideration, the Supreme Court was apparently to be a junior partner. It was therefore something of a bombshell when, in No. 78, Hamilton departed from a simple explication of the text of the Constitution and began to describe the Supreme Court's role in relation to the Congress. He pointed out that the judiciary must be a completely independent department and that this independence was required for political reasons. He wrote:

The complete independence of the courts of justice is peculiarly essential in a limited constitution. By a limited constitution, I understand one which contains certain specified exceptions to the legislative authority; such for instance, as that it shall pass no bills of attainder, no *ex post facto* laws, and the like. Limitations of this kind can be preserved in practice no other way than through the medium of courts of justice, whose duty it must be to declare all acts contrary to the manifest tenor of the constitution void. Without this, all the reservations of particular rights or privileges would amount to nothing. . . .

There is no position which depends on clearer principles than that every act of a delegated authority, contrary to the tenor of the commission under which it is exercised, is void. No legislative act, therefore, contrary to the constitution, can be valid. . . .

Where the will of the legislature, declared in its statutes, stands in opposition to that of the people, declared in the constitution, the judges ought to be governed by the latter rather than the former. They ought to regulate their decisions by the fundamental laws rather than by those which are not fundamental.

An appointed body of five men (nine men now), holding office for life, was to have the power to nullify acts passed by lawmakers elected by the people or their representatives. A nondemocratic tribunal, in other words, would be able to override the branch of government chosen by and responsible to the electorate. How could judicial supremacy be justified? Hamilton's reasoning was, first, that the Constitution was the "fundamental" law of the land and that its provisions stood on higher ground than any statutes passed by the legislature. And, second, he asserted that the Constitution, once adopted, would express the "real" will of the people. That is, acts of Congress might claim to represent the public will, but they might actually be expressing the transitory whims and momentary passions of the electorate. The Constitution, in contrast, embodied the enduring political values of the American nation.

Since the publication of No. 78 and the initial application of judicial review a decade and a half later by John Marshall in *Marbury v. Madison,* there has been endless debate on the powers of the judicial branch. Hamilton's prediction, in No. 81, was that members of the Supreme Court would be outstanding legal scholars, men "selected for their knowledge of the laws, acquired by long and laborious study." These men, presumably, would rise above partisan politics and the everyday clash of interests. They would, so it was supposed, interpret the Constitution coolly and dispassionately; and if they declared an act of Congress void they would do so because it clearly ran counter to the fundamental law as expressed in that document. But there is reason to suspect that there was more on Hamilton's mind than legal consistency. His interests were in establishing national authority and in encouraging industrial growth, and in all likelihood he intended that the Supreme Court would aid in this mission by overriding acts of a rural and agrarian Congress tempted to hamper these objectives. To be sure this strategy is not explicitly stated in *The Federalist,* but it can be inferred from Hamilton's major assumptions concerning the course of American development.

THE COURT'S CONSTITUENCY To challenge a popularly elected legislature requires both courage and power. From 1803 until 1937, the Supreme Court exercised Hamilton's mandate, striking down approximately 80 acts of Congress. It was able to do this largely because it had a series of powerful "constituencies" upon which it could rely for support. For even though it was an appointed body, the Supreme Court was able to gain support of important groups in society, which were prepared to defend its authority over that of the Congress. These constituencies were, first, the mercantile and financial interests of the Northeast, later the slaveholding interests of the South, and finally the burgeoning entrepreneurial interests that dominated the nation's economy from the close of the Civil War until the Depression of the 1930s. This was the kind of support Hamilton hoped would emerge for an independent judiciary. And in major particulars his forecast was a correct one for the first century and a half of the Republic's life. However, since the days of the New Deal the Supreme Court has been isolated rather than independent. It no longer has behind it a coherent and identifiable constituency; there is no major group of power and prestige to defend it against its detractors. For this reason it has had to scale down any political pretensions it might currently have.

Therefore it is not surprising that during the past several decades the Supreme Court has nullified few acts of Congress, and none of these have been significant statutes. It has exercised some control, for example, over the procedures employed in congressional investigations but it has not challenged the national legislative branch in the realm of public policy to any substantial extent. Rather the Court has pretty much confined its use of judicial review to nullifying acts of state legislatures. Many of these actions have had quite sweeping effects: particularly decisions dealing with racial segregation, legislative apportionment, and the rights of arrested persons. At the same time, most of the justices realize that were they to attempt to override the Congress on important issues, they would be faced with a counterattack against which they would have no effective defense. The isolation of the judicial branch is a serious development, and it is one of the unanticipated consequences of the fragmentation of power in American politics.

FREEDOM AND AUTHORITY

The proposed constitution sought to reconcile some of the major values facing modern government. The authors of *The Federalist* built their theory on a conception of society that was not beyond the powers of mortal men to attain. Madison was speaking both for himself and for Hamilton when he said in No. 51:

> But what is government itself but the greatest of all reflections on human nature? If men were angels, no government would be necessary. If angels were to govern men, neither external nor internal controls on government would be necessary. In framing a government which is to be administered by men over men, the great difficulty lies in this: you must first enable the government to control the governed; and in the next place oblige it to control itself.

Hamilton's great concern was to establish a government capable of controlling the governed, one that would allow for purposive and energetic leadership. His goal was to secure a strong national authority, and to this end he hoped to underpin the new republic with the support of a powerful class in society. Madison's concern, on the other hand, was to establish a government that would have the capacity for controlling itself. To achieve this objective, he defended the principles of federalism, separation of powers, and social pluralism. He was less interested in establishing a class base for the political system and more in seeing that a wide variety of interests were represented in the governmental process.

On a superficial reading it would seem that Hamilton's and Madison's aims could only run counter to each other. For would not Hamilton's goal of unified national power be upset by Madison's checks and balances and federal-state rivalries? The response must be that while differing in these important particulars, both *Federalist* authors were dedicated to the ideas of a united nation and individual freedom. But even on the question of freedom they were not wholly in agreement. For Hamilton, freedom spelled the right of the businessman to make money and invest it in productive enterprise. For Madison, it was the freedom of individuals and minorities to express their opinions and without having those rights abridged by an intolerant majority. Both authors shared misgivings about majority rule and the institutions of popular democracy. There can be no overlooking the tensions embodied in *The Federalist*. Indeed it was Madison himself, in No. 10, who said, "As long as the reason of man continues fallible, and he is at liberty to exercise it, different opinions will be formed."

REVIEW QUESTIONS

1. What were to be the functions and characteristics of the House of Representatives?

2. What is the "iron law of oligarchy"?

3. In what ways would the Senate differ from the House of Representatives?

4. What kind of men did Hamilton think ought to be selected for the Presidency?

5. In what sense was the Supreme Court to be the guardian of the Constitution?

6. Did Hamilton and Madison agree or differ in their fundamental aims?

8 THE JEFFERSONIAN REJOINDER

The new Constitution did not receive a unanimous welcome from the American people. In several states the document was ratified by only a slender margin, and at least one—Rhode Island—came close to rejecting it altogether. While many of these misgivings rose out of objections to specific provisions, not a few Americans felt uneasy over the general outlook of the framers. These dissenters held a quite different vision of the kind of society they wished America to become. Moreover, the questions they raised marked the beginnings of a conflict that continues into our own time. For there persist in this country some fundamental disagreements over the values and behavior most appropriate for the good life. The most vivid statement of an alternative outlook was enunciated by Thomas Jefferson.

It was perhaps just as well that Thomas Jefferson was out of the country while the Constitution was being drafted. His basic assumptions differed so deeply from those of Alexander Hamilton that, had he been present in Philadelphia, the debate might have become deadlocked in philosophical controversy. Nevertheless, Jefferson at first appeared willing to praise the new Constitution, calling it "unquestionably the wisest ever yet presented to men." Moreover, his opinion of *The Federalist* seemed equally enthusiastic. Those essays, he told Madison, comprised "the best commentary on the principles of government which ever was written." Yet whatever motives impelled these words of approval, the fact remains that Jefferson's views of human nature and the good society stood in marked contrast to those expressed by the *Federalist* authors.

Jefferson's philosophical position emerges from an examination of his widely ranging writings. These thoughts recur in his speeches, articles, and the voluminous correspondence he carried on with his compatriots of the day. This needs some emphasis if only because Jefferson's importance as a political theorist stems from these sources, and not from his conduct in public life. The gap between his ideas and his actions have been frequently commented upon. For example, he differed with Hamilton in taking a limited view of Presidential power. Yet when he himself occupied that office he negotiated the Louisiana Purchase, perhaps as expansive a use of Executive prerogative as the nation has ever witnessed. Jefferson's writings rank him as the foremost apostle of human liberty; however, he remained a slaveowner all of his life. He called for toleration toward disagreeable ideas, yet he expressed misgivings over the political leanings of faculty members at the University of Virginia. And some have added that while Jefferson styled himself a champion of the common man, his Monticello estate had one of the best wine cellars in the new nation.

But despite these apparent contradictions, Jefferson still produced a coherent body of ideas, which comprise a major strand in American political thought. Indeed, his enduring role in this country's history results more from the principles he enunciated than from his accomplishments as a politician. There is some justification, then, for dissociating Jefferson's writings from his performance as a partisan figure and public orficeholder. While such a separation may seem artificial, it may be recalled that the value of Jean-Jacques Rousseau's theories are not lessened by the fact that he walked out on his family, nor is John Stuart Mill's stature as a philosopher affected by his affection for another man's wife.

A SELF-CORRECTING CITIZENRY

Most textbooks describe the differences between Hamilton and Jefferson in terms of the one's supporting a strong central government while the other favored relegating power to the several states. While this juxtaposition is certainly true, their disagreements ran far deeper. For Jefferson rejected the doctrine of original sin; he espoused majority rule; and his conception of how men might best live together stood in sharp variance not only to Hamilton's assumptions but most of Madison's as well.

HUMAN REASON "I am persuaded myself that the good sense of the people will always be found to be the best army," Jefferson wrote. "They may be led astray for a moment, but will soon correct themselves." The average citizen, he believed, is a rational individual. He may occasionally succumb to selfish or shortsighted appeals by politicians; however, his capacity for reflection can be relied upon to return him to responsible paths of conduct. To Jefferson's mind, the people did not need to be protected from themselves. If they sometimes revealed the attributes so feared by Hamilton—"ambition," "avarice," "passion," "vindictiveness," and the rest—he saw much less evidence of those traits than did the *Federalist* authors. Put very simply, Jefferson perceived a substantially higher quotient of reason in human beings and consequently was suspicious of granting governmental authority to small circles of officeholders who allegedly comprehended the public interest better than citizens did themselves.

Hence Jefferson's conviction that "man may be governed by truth and reason." His own encounters with the American people convinced him that more harm than good would come from attempting to shield them from facts they might misunderstand or ideas they might misinterpret. "The discernment that they have manifested between truth and falsehood," he wrote, "shows that they may be safely trusted to hear everything true and false, and form correct judgments between them." At least two corollaries follow from this conclusion. The first is that there should be no censorship of expression. For "false" ideas will fall of their own weight due to the public's capacity for seeing through faulty logic and specious facts. Jefferson would allow unlimited liberty of speech, publication, and other attempts at persuasion. The alternative would be to permit some powerful individuals to decide what the public may or may not hear.

THE IMPORTANCE OF EDUCATION   The accompanying inference was to favor majority rule. The various devices in the Constitution—such as indirect election of senators or an electoral college to select the President—held little appeal for Jefferson. In his judgment, popular participation could be counted on to produce wise policies and sober statesmen. At the same time, he understood that so pervasive a public involvement would require a continual effort at education. "No one more sincerely wishes the spread of information among mankind than I do," he wrote, "and none has greater confidence in its effect toward supporting free and good government." Given that connection, he could say:

> Educate and inform the whole mass of the people. Enable them to see that it is in their interest to preserve peace and order, and they will preserve them. . . . They are the only sure reliance for the preservation of our liberty. After all, it is my principle that the will of the majority should prevail.

What of the prospect, so disquieting to both Madison and Hamilton, that majority rule might become transformed into majority tyranny? Jefferson's reply was that while constitutional protections might be necessary to safeguard the rights of minorities, the best insurance would be to educate the public to appreciate the value of toleration. Thus he felt that majority rule need not stand in opposition to minority freedoms. "Though the will of the majority is in all cases to prevail, that will to be rightful must be reasonable," he explained. "The minority possess their equal rights which equal law must protect, and to violate would be oppression." In other words, a rational citizenry would exercise self-restraint. While possessing the capacity to ride roughshod over defense-less minorities or dissenting individuals, the majority would refrain from using its power in these ways. This, at least, was Jefferson's presumption. If it is noted that America's white majority has not been altogether tolerant of minorities having other colorations or that the country's heterosexual majority has shown little tendency to protect those of alternative inclinations, Jefferson's reply would probably be that our efforts at public education have been less than wholehearted. Oppressive acts, he would say, arise from ignorance and are not due to any inherent perversities in human nature.

"CREATED EQUAL" Support for majority rule implies a belief in human equality as well. If 51 plumbers are to be allowed to outvote 49 physicists, then the premise must be that a plumber's opinions are of equal value to those of a physicist. However, more than simply equality of opinions is involved in the Jeffersonian outlook. "All men are created equal," was the first of the "truths" which Jefferson held to be "self-evident" in the Declaration of Independence. Equality at creation really means that all of us are born pretty much the same kind of creatures. Such differences as emerge subsequent to our birth result almost entirely from the varying experiences and advantages that individuals encounter in the course of growing up. This position requires some clarification. To begin with, Jefferson's perception entails giving far greater stress to environmental factors than to genetic inheritance. If we perceive some people as smarter, abler, or more attractive than others, this is largely because they were raised in surroundings that placed a premium on such attributes. While some traits may be explained by the transmission of parental genes, they do not make some babies "superior" to others. Indeed, to paraphrase the earlier quotation: "all babies are created equal." Moreover, if societies do discover differentials among individuals—for example, in "intelligence"—that is because societies themselves draw up tests that end up giving some people higher ratings than others. And if there are rich and poor, it is because certain economic systems pay more to people who appear to fulfill particular functions. Indeed, the attainment or possession of attributes such as warmth or affection or generosity may not be rewarded at all or even be used as a measure of personal quality. Thus the entire Jeffersonian persuasion carries deep misgivings not only about grading people, but also over the competitions wherein some are said to succeed while others fail. We are, in this view, all equal—until, that is, someone intervenes to give us grades on our appearance or performance.

And whereas Hamilton took the position that every nation contains only a limited measure of talent and virtue, Jefferson held the view that these and other praiseworthy qualities distribute themselves widely throughout the population. To Hamilton's mind, the government should provide special protection, encouragement, and power to those individuals who play more productive roles in society. As far as Jefferson was concerned, every citizen shares in the attributes common to humanity and for this reason should be permitted to participate on an equal plane.

A DEFENSE OF DEFIANCE   An emphasis on order and the argument for governmental authority did not figure strongly in Jefferson's outlook. As has been indicated, Hamilton sought to establish a "firm union" to serve as a barrier against what he chose to call "domestic faction and insurrection." Apparently, Jefferson was less troubled by the prospect of rebellion. "If the happiness of the mass of the people can be secured at the expense of a little tempest now and then, or even of a little blood, it will be a precious purchase," he wrote. In other words, he assigned higher priority to values other than order. Stability can not only induce stagnation, he believed, but too serene a society may lead people to settle for a more limited life than they might otherwise know. Referring to Shays' rebellion, he said:

> God forbid we should ever be twenty years without such a rebellion. The people cannot be all, and always, well-informed. The part which is wrong will be discontented in proportion to the importance of the facts they misconceive. If they remain quiet under such misconceptions, it is a lethargy, the forerunner of death to the public liberty. . . . What signify a few lives lost in a century or two? The tree of liberty must be refreshed from time to time with the blood of patriots and tyrants.

Jefferson seems to be saying at least two things in this statement. On the one hand, he is suggesting that resistance may stem from misconceptions—from people's failure to inform themselves adequately on the purposes of policies they perceive as objectionable. Here, presumably, Jefferson would call for more strenuous efforts to educate public opinion. But he also indicates that rebellion is preferable to an unquestioning attitude which always accepts authority. For that mentality, even if it produces peace, encourages both political apathy and intellectual stupor. Thus the sustenance of liberty depends on an active citizenry, even if this results in occasional rebellions based on ignorance or emotional outbursts. Bloodshed should not necessarily be deplored. To Jefferson, it was a sign that people were in fact concerned about the conditions confronting them. Better "a few lives lost" than a sluggish submission to whatever powers predominate. "A little rebellion now and then is a good thing," he concluded. "It is a medicine necessary for the sound health of government." If citizens accept as sufficient the standards prevailing in their time, they will have little inducement to inquire whether life might conceivably be made better.

THE HAMILTONIAN PROPOSALS

In order to secure a perspective on Jefferson's idea of the good society, it would be well to outline the tendencies he found most disturbing. As might be guessed, many of these tenets were contained in Hamilton's economic proposals, which called for increasing industrialization, expanded cities, and the encouragement of entrepreneurial activity. Not only did Hamilton wish to see the United States become an impressive international power; he also saw the means to that end in technological innovation. This vision foresaw a hardworking population, motivated by the rewards an expanding economy might offer. All this Hamilton set down in his "Report on the Subject of Manufactures" which, as Secretary of the Treasury, he submitted to President Washington in December of 1791. The purpose of those passages was to enlighten the Chief Executive of a predominantly agricultural nation as to the advantages to be gained through new productive processes.

INDUSTRY AND THE INDIVIDUAL Hamilton's first argument concerned "productivity," a concept not yet in common usage and which therefore required an elementary explanation. "The employment of machinery forms an item of great importance in the general mass of national industry," he wrote. "It is an artificial force brought in aid of the natural force of man; and, to all the purposes of labor, is an increase of hands and accession of strength." If the labor force turns increasingly to factory work, output will rise from the efficiencies of mechanized methods. "Those occupations which give greatest use of this auxiliary," Hamilton went on, "contribute most to the general stock of industrious effort and, in consequence, to the general product of industry." His proposal, in short, was to lure people off their farms and into employments where they would be more productive.

However, Hamilton was not interested merely in getting more work out of people. He also believed that the world of industry offered individuals the opportunity to discover their aptitudes and potentialities. Participation in manufacturing processes, he said, provides "greater scope for the diversity of talents and dispositions which discriminate men from each other." Thus the advent of industrialization would "cherish and stimulate the activity of the human mind by multiplying the objects of enterprise." For:

> Minds of the strongest and most active powers . . . fall below mediocrity and labor without effect if confined to uncongenial pursuits. And it is thence to be inferred that the results of human exertion may be immensely increased by diversifying its objects. When all the different kinds of industry obtain in a community, each individual can find his proper element, and can call into activity the whole vigor of his nature.

Hamilton, no less than Jefferson, was fearful of any tendencies to lethargy on the part of the public. Like Jefferson, he wanted to bring out the best in people and keep them on their toes at all times. But whereas Jefferson's chief focus was on intellectual activity, Hamilton's concern centered on dedication to one's job. Jefferson would have inquiring minds address themselves to political and cultural issues; Hamilton would apply the public intelligence to industrial productivity and economic innovation.

THE MATERIALIST MENTALITY Hence Hamilton envisaged a society where everyone would involve himself in the productive process. He anticipated "moonlighting," not only because factories would often need help at odd hours, but also because people would want extra cash to buy the new products emerging from an industrial economy:

> In places where manufacturing institutions prevail, besides the persons regularly engaged in them, they afford occasional and extra employment to industrious individuals and families, who are willing to devote the leisure resulting from the intermissions of their ordinary pursuits to collateral labors, as a resource for multiplying their acquisitions or their enjoyments.

The acquisitive and materialist mentality did not trouble Hamilton. Rather, he saw it as a means of keeping people occupied and active. Nor was he worried that these developments might weaken other institutions in society. Indeed he commented that under his proposals, "women and children are rendered more useful, and the latter more early useful, by manufacturing establishments than they would otherwise be." To him, putting women and children to work seemed a splendid idea. He exhibited no qualms over the consequences this might have for family life as traditionally conceived. If Jefferson saw nothing wrong with political revolutions, Hamilton was advocating nothing less than a thoroughgoing industrial transformation—one which would, as it turned out, have deeper and more far-reaching consequences for American society than the various political upheavals this country was to experience.

JEFFERSON'S COUNTERPROPOSAL

Jefferson did not mount an explicit rejoinder to Hamilton's "Report on the Subject of Manufactures." His sentiments on this general subject actually appeared several years earlier in his *Notes on Virginia,* a pamphlet he wrote while serving in Paris as Minister to France. The importance of these reflections lies not in any attempt to refute Hamilton's economic arguments, but rather in describing the setting which would encourage the best in human capacities.

Only the agricultural life, Jefferson argued, can bring out the qualities needed for constructive citizenship, social tolerance, and intellectual growth. The fewer the farmers a society has, the less will free government flourish. "The proportion which the other classes of citizens bears to that of its husbandmen," Jefferson wrote, "is the proportion of its unsound to its healthy parts, and is a good enough barometer whereby to measure its degree of corruption." Given the belief that man is naturally good, the experience of history shows that this goodness may be corrupted by temptations that bring out the selfish side of human character. Therefore Jefferson's hope was that Americans could be shielded from inducements and occupations that warp men's judgments and emphasize their differences. For this reason, he opposed industrialization, which would lure people off the countryside. "While we have land to labor," he advised, "let us never wish our citizens occupied at a workbench." In fact, Jefferson went so far as to propose that the United States build no factories at all—the direct opposite of the Hamiltonian program—but rather import manufactured goods from abroad. "For the general operation of manufacture, let our workshops remain in Europe," he said. Of course this would be costly in economic terms:

> It is better to carry provisions and materials to workmen there, than to bring them to the provisions and materials, and with them their manners and principles. The loss by the transportation of commodities across the Atlantic will be made up in the happiness and permanence of government.

THE CASE AGAINST CITIES   Indeed Jefferson seemed not a little fearful of the workers who might immigrate to America were this country to embark on industrialization. Such individuals (he did not mention specific nationalities) might not possess the "manners and principles" necessary for the political and cultural climate Jefferson wished to create. Thus he preferred the added expense involved in sending American raw materials to Europe, having them processed there, with the finished products shipped back to the United States. Better to pay this price than to risk an infusion of persons whose very presence could jeopardize the American experiment. This is not to say that Jefferson felt that all "foreigners" were inherently incapable of self-government. Rather he suspected that they would cluster in cities, where they would be more susceptible to political manipulation and less apt to exercise their rational faculties. It is also worth noting another reason why the higher cost of manufactured goods did not trouble Jefferson. The cheaper such commodities might be, the more Americans might develop materialist habits and acquisitive instincts. A rudimentary and self-sufficient life in rural surroundings may provide fewer creature comforts. However, too plentiful an availability of possessions can corrupt character and deflect attention from more important ends in life.

Concluding his analysis, Jefferson made quite explicit his assumptions concerning the demography of democracy:

> The mobs of great cities add just so much to the support of pure government as sores do to the strength of the human body. It is the manner and spirit of a people which preserve a republic in vigor. A degeneracy in these is a canker which soon eats to the heart of its laws and constitution.

How can a writer like Jefferson speak of people as a "mob"? Particularly after all the things he had said about the good sense of the average citizen? To characterize people as "sores" or "cankers" seems a far remove from his earlier explication of human nature. The answer, of course, is that while all men and women have the potential for altruism, this capacity will be crushed by the pressures of urban life. In other words, the emergence of a benign nature depends on its being nurtured in a setting conducive to its flowering. Persons who might be sturdy and intelligent individualists in the country would, if placed amid the congestion and competition of a city, give vent to selfishness and impetuosity. By the same token, a member of the urban "mob" would, had he been raised in rural surroundings, behave as a rational and responsible citizen. Jefferson's point, therefore, is that a theory of human nature must be accompanied by some delineation of the social environment most conducive to developing these traits and tendencies.

A COMMUNITY OF EQUALS   Jefferson never elaborated on the social structure he sought to create. Yet the impression cannot help but arise that it would be a simple society, lacking class lines and clashing interests. Its people would comprise a community committed to common goals and a shared conception of the good life. At the same time, all issues would be open to full discussion, with everyone participating in public life. Power in such a society would not rest with unchallenged centers of authority, but would rather rely on citizens having an informed understanding of existing realities and available options. Thus there is reason to suspect that Jefferson would have accepted the depiction provided by Jean-Jacques Rousseau:

> There are no embroilments or conflicts of interest; the common good is everywhere clearly apparent, and only good sense is needed to perceive it. Men who are upright and simple are difficult to deceive because of their simplicity; lures and ingenious pretexts fail to impose upon them. Among the happiest people in the world, bands of peasants are seen regulating affairs of state under an oak, and always acting wisely. Can we help scorning the methods of other nations, which make themselves illustrious and wretched with so much art and mystery?

The issue, then, has been joined. Hamilton felt that the tempo and complexity of city life would bring out the best in people. Jefferson saw that experience as fostering a "degeneracy" of the human spirit. Obviously, the controversy here transcends the case for or against cities. The problem, further, is to clarify a conception of human possibilities and then to silhouette a setting where these attributes may develop to their fullest advantage. The antagonism between Jefferson and Hamilton reflects a debate that began long before the birth of the American republic and that will continue until a verdict of human history finally validates one or the other of these positions.

REVIEW QUESTIONS

1. Under what conditions and circumstances will majorities refrain from using their full powers?

2. What interpretations can be given to the phrase "all men are created equal"?

3. When is defiance to be desired over obedience?

4. How does industrialization affect the personality of a population?

5. If man has an intrinsic "nature," why does his behavior change as he moves from one set of surroundings to another?

6. Where and in what ways are the Hamiltonian and Jeffersonian outlooks expressed in contemporary American society?

FOR FURTHER READING

THE STUDY OF POLITICS

Catlin, George: *Systematic Politics,* University of Toronto Press, Toronto, Canada, 1962.

Easton, David: *A Systems Analysis of Political Life,* John Wiley & Sons, Inc., New York, 1965.

Eulau, Heinz: *The Behavioral Persuasion in Politics,* Random House, Inc., New York, 1963.

Storing, Herbert (ed.): *Essays on the Scientific Study of Politics,* Holt, Rinehart & Winston, Inc., New York, 1962.

Van Dyke, Vernon: *Political Science: A Philosophical Analysis,* Stanford University Press, Stanford, Calif., 1960.

THE WESTERN TRADITION

Hacker, Andrew: *Political Theory: Philosophy, Ideology, Science,* The Macmillan Company, New York, 1961.

Sabine, George: *A History of Political Theory,* Holt, Rinehart & Winston, Inc., New York, 1961.

Strauss, Leo: *What is Political Philosophy?* The Free Press, New York, 1959.

Wolin, Sheldon: *Politics and Vision,* Little, Brown and Company, Boston, 1960.

AMERICAN ORIGINS

Brant, Irving: *James Madison: Father of the Constitution,* The Bobbs-Merrill Co., Inc., Indianapolis, 1950.

Dietze, Gottfried: *The Federalist: A Classic of Federalism and Free Government,* The Johns Hopkins Press, Baltimore, 1960.

Hacker, Louis M.: *Alexander Hamilton in the American Tradition,* McGraw-Hill Book Company, New York, 1957.

Padover, Saul (ed.): *Thomas Jefferson on Democracy,* Mentor Books, New York, 1939.

Rossiter, Clinton: *1787: The Grand Convention,* The Macmillan Company, New York, 1966.

AMERICAN INSTITUTIONS

Bickel, Alexander: *The Supreme Court and the Idea of Progress,* Harper & Row, Publishers, 1970.

Egger, Rowland: *The President of the United States,* 2d ed., McGraw-Hill Book Company, New York, 1972.

Harris, Joseph: *Congress and the Legislative Process,* McGraw-Hill Book Company, New York, 1972.

Huitt, Ralph, and Robert Peabody: *Congress: Two Decades of Analysis,* Harper & Row, Publishers, New York, 1969.

Johnson, Donald, and Jack Walker (eds.): *The Dynamics of the American Presidency,* John Wiley & Sons, Inc., New York, 1964.

Mason, Alpheus, and William Beaney: *The Supreme Court in a Free Society,* Prentice-Hall, Inc., Englewood Cliffs, N.J., 1969.

INDEX